Lord, Change Me

LORD, CHANGE ME

EVELYN CHRISTENSON

assisted editorially by Viola Blake

EVELYN CHRISTENSON is Chairman of the Board of United Prayer Ministry, Minneapolis, Minnesota, and speaks frequently at retreats, conventions, and seminars on the subject of prayer.

OTHER BOOKS BY EVELYN CHRISTENSON
A Study Guide for Evangelism Praying
Praying God's Way
What Happens When Women Pray
What Happens When We Pray For Our Families
Gaining Through Losing
What Happens When God Answers Prayer
What GOD Does When Women Pray
What Happens When Children Pray
Battling the Prince of Darkness
  Rescuing Captives from Satan's Kingdom

For further information visit:
www.EvelynChristensonMinistries.com

ISBN: 978-0-9817467-0-8

Contents

*T*o my dear husband, Chris, for wanting God's will for me rather than his own, and for his patience and love during the long hours of producing this book.

and

To my dear children, Jan, Nancy, and Kurt, who have given to me the privilege of motherhood, without which many of these lessons could never have been learned.

*I*NTRODUCTION

*O*ther than my prayer accepting Jesus as my Savior and Lord, my most life changing prayer continues to be "Lord, change me." And since being published as a book in 1968, people are still saying to me today, "*Lord, Change Me* is the most important book I've ever read. It completely changed my life." Just yesterday a young unmarried mother of two said that she is devouring it page by page because she needs so badly the message it brings.

The success and impact of this book over the years has surprised me! The book's title can be very threatening—an open challenge to our 'me-ism' culture of "I can do it myself, thank you." There was a time in the beginning when I expected readers to reject the book with the attitude "I know I need to change, but I don't want somebody telling me about it!" We all seem to want the other person to change to solve all of our own problems.

At first readers may have been curious, surprised, intrigued, defensive, or sometimes resentful at the suggestion that letting the Lord change them first actually would change those they were trying to change. But for 23 years now, readers have told me how thrilled they were at the amazing transformation in themselves, and the desired changes—immediate or eventual—which occurred in those they were trying in vain to change. They too, have discovered the secret to changed relationships—Lord, change *me*. Now with more than a million copies of *Lord, Change Me* in print, I am more convinced than ever that God wants His secret for my readers, too.

It's a simple prayer—just three words "Lord … change … me." Each word forms one of the three sections of the book. But part of the secret to the success of this prayer is the order in which the three words are addressed. I have taught from this book on every continent and I always have reversed its three words, starting with its secret: "Why Me? Why not my husband? Why not my children? Why not my boss, my friend, you? Why ME?"

I struggled alone with God for 14 months, asking Him to change me—not anybody else. But suddenly and spontaneously it was not just for me. My very private journey became a journey for those women I was leading as a pastor's wife. Then it gained momentum. Others started asking about this life-changing prayer, and I began sharing at retreats, conferences, Bible studies, teacher-training sessions, church prayer weeks, and Sunday school classes in our country and Canada. So *Lord, Change Me* was born—a book that God continues to use in all those ways around the world today.

I continue to pray "Lord, change me" for myself, as I have prayed in some form at least once a day since that first prayer in 1968. The process is as timeless as the God who gave it to me. Change for change's sake just to try something new can be beneficial or disastrous. But, when the goal of change is to being conformed to the image of God's dear Son Jesus, the concept is as foolproof as God, its author. The needed changes He has shown me have produced repentance, humility, and obedience—all exchanging my will for His perfect holy will.

Section 1 of this book starts with the secret word "me"; and God's changes have resulted in a tremendously deep and intimate walk with God, in incredible open doors on every continent, and in startling changes in others even while I was concentrating just on me.

After praying that initial prayer, I found I had to ask God *how* He wanted to change me. Section 2 teaches the seven methods He used. The first four are from His Word, the Bible. Since God is the only author who is always present with us while we read, I continuously find my heart burning within me like the two on the Emmaus Road when the risen Savior joined them and opened the Scriptures to them. God promised all the wisdom His children ever would need for a transformed lifestyle. In all the times I have used this method myself devotionally, and then for retreats and even in huge conferences, God has never failed to speak.

We also are changed as we study His Word, the only absolutely trustworthy source of truth. Then, amazingly, when we don't have a Bible around, the Holy Spirit recalls the Scripture we have hidden in our hearts—right when we need it to change us for the better.

The other three methods the Lord uses to change me are through prayer. The first, "When I Ask Him," is my admitting my need to be changed, and God always hears and answers in ways I never expected—or never even knew I needed.

"When I pray for others" is the second prayer method. I am amazed at how I cannot gossip about or hate someone and pray for him or her at the same time. And I am the one who is gently—or sometimes drastically—changed by the Lord as I stay in His presence in prayer for someone else.

I have proven the last method of "When others pray for me" through 30 years of being supported by my telephone prayer chains, national 24 hour prayer clocks, prayer calendars and letters, friends, and my praying board. Those around me are constantly amazed at the strength God gives me in spite of horrendous schedules and physical limitations. But I sincerely believe it is God who has provided all the strength, wisdom, and guidance—because of their awesome faithfulness when I admit to them I have a need for God to change me. And the result is always for the better.

However, God showed me a danger in this process—and an unsettling truth. It was not always Himself "the Lord" doing the changing. According to James 3:15, there are three other sources vying for my thoughts and actions, changing me. Section 3 of this book deals with the subtle or deliberate ways we are changed by other people, by our own sensual selves, by demons, and not by God. The test of which source of wisdom we have heeded is the result it produces in us—whether or not we are changed more and more into our goal of conforming to the likeness of Jesus.

Without my naming it, I have been praying for the Lord to change me all my life. Since praying for God to forgive my sins and Jesus to come into my heart as my Savior, I have been praying in many, many ways for the Lord to change me. But in 1968 God showed me "Lord, change me" praying as the secret of relationships with other people and how my changing first in that relationship would be used by God to influence how He wants them to change.

This book was written for you, dear reader, so you can know the secret too. Through these seven simple biblical principles, you can discover your incredible potential for a deeper walk with God—and the joy of changed relationships with other people.

Now that this process from God has passed the test of time, I can tell you that I absolutely know it works!

Evelyn Christenson
January 2002

SECTION I

Me

1

Why Me?

*L*ord, I will never speak again—never—if this is the price my husband has to pay for my being a public speaker." And I wept as I prayed, "Lord, I want You to change me into the kind of wife *You* want me to be."

I had crept out of bed at 5:30 A.M. to seek the Lord in my private "prayer closet" by my old green chair. And as the minutes ticked into hours, I stayed on my knees struggling.

Why was I telling God I would never speak again? Was I disappointed, disillusioned, tired out? Oh, no—just the opposite. Flooding over me as I agonized with God was the enormity of what I was promising. I was willing to give up a way of life to which I was sure He had called me: my weekly women's neighborhood Bible study, the large adult Sunday School class—one of the greatest joys of my life—I had been teaching for almost twelve years, and my busy banquet-speaking schedule. Then my mind turned to all the retreats in the United States and Canada, where I had seen God work in such quiet, yet powerful, ways. I thought of the Vacation Bible Schools, teacher-training classes, conferences, conventions, etc. The list parading through my mind seemed endless. But I prayed, "Yes, Lord, *all!*"

My husband Chris missed me, and suddenly I was aware of his footsteps on the stairs. He paused halfway down and asked, "May I join you?" I looked up at him and sobbed, "Chris, I'm not praying for *you*, I'm praying for *me*! I'm praying that the Lord will change *me*." (The Lord may have had some changing to do in Chris' life, but that was not *my* concern that morning. That was between the Lord and Chris.)

WHY ME, LORD?

But why did I need to be changed? Hadn't I cried over all my sins one Sunday afternoon when I was only nine years old? I had heard evangelist Harry McCormick Lintz preach in church that morning in Muskegon, Michigan, and I thought the evening service would never come—and then that it would never end—so eager was I to invite Jesus into my heart. I almost ran down the aisle, then opened my heart completely to Jesus as our Sunday School superintendent knelt beside me and carefully explained from the Scriptures how I could become a Christian.

And hadn't I really made Him *Lord* in addition to Savior that Sunday? Yes, I had. From that day on I had grown steadily—sometimes in little baby steps and at other times in giant steps of faith—but always I had wanted and sought His will. Hadn't I even spent months praying about my first and only boyfriend until I was positive he was the one God wanted me to marry? And hadn't Chris and I, as engaged students at Moody Bible Institute, spent our free moments poring over Walter A. Maier's *For Better Not for Worse*, the Christian classic in those days for brides and grooms who wanted a Christ-centered marriage? And hadn't I, in agreement with my husband, sought only God's will as we struggled to find His spot for us in full-time Christian service, and later as we served Him as pastor and wife for sixteen years? Yes, I had.

And in that last pastorate hadn't I spent six miserable weeks confessing sins to God with Lorna and Signe, my two prayer partners, before He released us to pursue our goal—prayer for our church? Hadn't God given us three years of deep intercessory prayer? And hadn't He done a Herculean job *in* and *on* and *through* us as the women of our church experimented in our "What Happens When Women Pray" project?

SO, THEN WHY ME?

My personal agony early that morning by my old green chair was precipitated by what had happened at our denomination's annual conference in Davenport the week before. It was June 1968, and I was flying high. The previous fall, the national committee of our denomination had asked me to do a project for the Crusade of the Americas: "Working with women in your own church, would you discover in a six-month period *what happens when women pray?*" * I had accepted the challenge with enthusiasm. Now I had a fantastic report to give to the 600 women attending the opening banquet of our conference. Women from all over the United States and Canada, as well as foreign missionaries, would hear the results of our six-month experiment. Just before the banquet started, a man carrying what looked like a movie camera arrived and said to me, "Wave your arms and make believe you're speaking." As I complied, our national director, sitting at my right, whispered laughingly out of the corner of her mouth, "Psst, I think that's a TV camera!" And I was horrified to discover that she was right!

Early the next morning the jabs started—not at me, but at my husband—from fellow pastors and friends. "Hey, I saw your wife on TV. Wow!" To my horror, the local TV station had chosen the segment showing my pseudo-speech to represent our entire national conference on its news telecast. All week long Chris had borne the brunt of this cruel teasing. It became so embarrassing that I was the most crushed wife you could possibly imagine when we left the conference. I arrived home in Rockford, brokenhearted and puzzled. That is what had brought me to my knees beside my old green chair.

*Read *What Happens When Women Pray*, by Evelyn Christenson, for a complete report of this project. Published by Cook Communications Ministries, Colorado Springs, CO 80918.

WHY NOT VICTORY DAY?

All through breakfast that same morning, the first Tuesday in July, and while dressing for our women's weekly prayer meeting at Alpine Park, I kept dabbing away the tears. Even as I drove to the park I kept telling myself, "This is victory day, and we are going to have a victory celebration." But the tears persisted—not tears of joy, but tears of brokenness.

Eagerly the pray-ers gathered, waiting expectantly to hear what had happened in Davenport. These were the women with whom I had experimented in prayer the previous six months. These were the women, their ranks now multiplied, who had pled daily with God during the whole week I was in Davenport, that He would undergird me and that what they had experienced would spread to other women.

I felt strongly that these women waiting at Alpine Park deserved to know what had happened in those six months when *they* prayed—that after I shared, every one of the 600 women present at the banquet stood to her feet and promised God that she would go home and start proving that God does answer "when women pray." They deserved to learn the outcome of their praying as they arbitrarily picked out one of the conference speakers to zero in on in prayer. I wanted to tell them that after he had spoken I had followed him into the wing of the platform area and asked, "Rev. Hanstad, would you tell me how it was preaching out there today? You see, our ladies in Rockford picked you from among all the conference speakers as a special subject of prayer for many days. Did it make a difference?" He drew a quick breath and said, "Oh, I've never had such *freedom*. I'm usually so uptight and nervous when I speak before all my peers and those administrators, but today it was different. I felt so free; there was no tension at all."

These women who had prayed for me so faithfully while I was in Davenport also deserved to know that I had awakened on the morning of the banquet with a burning sore throat and a throbbing, stuffy head. I had been too sick to pray for myself. All I could do was mumble weakly from my bed. "Oh, God, tell somebody to pray; tell somebody to pray." And without knowing of my condition, these women who were waiting in the park had prayed all that day for me. They deserved to know that God had heard and answered their prayers, for after I had crawled out of bed to get ready for the banquet that evening, still unable to talk out loud or breathe freely, a miracle had happened. I had bent over to brush my teeth, and, when I raised my head, I was well. My voice was normal, my head was clear, the sore throat and miserable aching had disappeared.

I had planned the victory speech they deserved. Their six-month job was done. But God had further plans. He was leading us up the next rung of the spiritual ladder. He had already started the process in me, bringing me down to the depths of despair that I might rise to something higher. He had some more changing to do in me. So, instead of the victory speech, I told them the whole story of what had transpired earlier that morning by my old green chair.

Trying to hide my stubborn tears, I shared the pain of my experience with the women. They all wept with me. We were feeling an unexpected and different kind of victory. I remember Katy praying that morning, "Lord, I don't care what it is, take it from me so that I can serve You effectively. Lord, I don't care what it is." Now, Katy is a sharp gal. Her husband is a tennis champion, and they have two beautiful children. She is one of those women you watch to find out what the styles are going to be next year. But Katy wept along with the rest of us that morning as we prayed, "Lord, change me." Our hearts were all echoing her prayer, "O God, take away anything—so that You can really use me." Katy desperately wanted God to be first in her life.

But a strange thing happened. Following that meeting, and for over a year afterward, we never used the phrase, "Lord, change me." It was to go underground, to emerge fourteen months later.

A NEW PROCESS

God didn't take me up on my offer to give up my speaking and teaching, but He did begin that day to answer my prayer, "Lord, change me." He already had the next step in my spiritual maturity planned and ready for me. He started that morning to teach me a great principle and began a process in my life that is still at work. I have discovered through the years that surprising things happen when I pray, "Lord, change *me*—don't change my husband, don't change my children, don't change my pastor, change *me!*" This doesn't mean that I approve or even condone everything they do, but rather that I concentrate on how I handle my actions and reactions. More and more the fact comes into focus that they, and not I, are responsible before God for their actions. But I am responsible for the changes that need to be made in *me.*

This concept became the process whereby Evelyn was to become more Christ-like, conformed to *His* image, as stated in Romans 8:29, "For whom He did foreknow, He also did predestinate *to be conformed to the image of His Son.*" And since being Christ-like is my goal, I must expect this process to continue throughout my life and end only "when He shall appear" and I shall be "like Him" (1 John 3:2).

Although it was to be fourteen months before the "Lord,—change—me" concept was to be shared, the process had started. God had launched me personally on a fourteen-month gestation period. The "birth" would not take place until over a year later. This was the process of facing the reality of *my* need to change—again and again.

The struggle was like a hot iron inside me. That's the only way I can describe it. And it took fourteen solid months of turning to the only adequate, worthy Source of change—God Himself—and of searching His Word, allowing Him to make changes in my life, not in anybody else's.

"O God," I kept praying, "don't change anybody else, not my husband, not my children, just change ME!"

ME AGAIN?

That same June, I had some more changes to make. (What a horrible month that was!) I discovered something new about myself—because my daughter told me!

At the dinner table one evening Jan, our just-turned-eighteen eldest, abruptly announced, "Mother, I don't ever want to hear your philosophy again. Do you know that the tone of your voice actually changes when you start giving your philosophy? I know what's coming every single time."

"*Me* again?" I pushed my chair from the table, flew up to my bedroom and threw myself, sobbing, on my bed.

What was God teaching me *this* time? Jan always had been an independent first child, determinedly doing her own thing—following the encyclopedia's instructions for formal table settings while still in second grade; conquering the world of reading in sixth grade by winning our denomination's national reading contest. Her "I-can-do-it-myself-Mother" personality had been there from birth, but always under mother's guidance. So what was happening to her now? What had legally becoming an adult at her eighteenth birthday done to her?

Then, agonizing in my soul, I prayed, "Lord, don't change Jan. I know she's a teenager who needs to find her way in the world. Just change me! Lord, make me the kind of mother You want me to be. O God, I know she's growing up. Show me, please, how You want *me* to change!"

Then began in earnest what was to stretch into fourteen months of soul-searching for me.

WITHOUT A WORD

As I looked in the Bible for direction, God gave me a *principle* from 1 Peter 3:1–2 that guided my "changing" and carried me through those difficult fourteen months. At that time the emphasis for me from God was that others were to *observe my* chaste and reverent behavior. "So that some ... may be won *without a word*" (RSV).

Although this verse speaks specifically of the husband-wife relationship, I was to find that the "without-a-word" principle also worked with mothers and daughters. I determined not to impose my philosophy on Jan again. No more "preachy" mother!

Keeping my advice to myself, especially with my personality, wasn't easy. And Jan even enrolled at my alma mater as a freshman that fall! Oh, how I could have helped her by telling her just how to do everything. After all, hadn't I spent seven years with her daddy on that campus (and with her as a little baby)? And hadn't I, as secretary to the president, typed the disciplinary letters to parents and worked with the details of scholarships and college administration? But I restrained myself from offering my help. She didn't want it. Her independent attitude prevailed. She had to find out who *she* was—by herself.

I've learned since that that time wasn't easy for Jan either. She has confided to me that frequently, those first few weeks, she would sit in her dorm, bite her lip, and blink hard to keep back the tears—determined not to call home every time she felt lonely—determined to become independent—determined to make her own decisions in college. And at the same time I was sitting home just as determined—blinking back my tears—to let her find her own philosophy of life, to find her own way in the world.

When the first child turns eighteen and decides to cut the apron strings, parents (especially mothers) almost bleed to death. Their wounds seem to be much deeper than those of the children, and heal so much more slowly. Letting go of Jan was one of the most devastating things that had ever happened to me. How I thank God for five years of preparation before our next child became of age. I didn't bleed nearly so much, for I had had five years to change my "smotherhood" to "motherhood." And Nancy could walk with much more confidence in the field that Jan had plowed as virgin soil those many years before.

IT WORKS

By February following that horrible June, my then eight months of silence about my philosophy was starting to bring results, although I honestly wasn't looking for them. I was only concentrating on the Lord changing me. That He might in turn be changing my daughter hadn't occurred to me. Our first visit to her college was for Founder's Week. As we sat conversing at dinner with Jan and the boy she was then dating, I sat in stunned silence as she carefully, deliberately kept saying to him, "My mother thinks this about that. And she thinks this about that." The other part of those verses in 1 Peter 3 was proving to be true, "That some … *may be won* … when they [observe] your reverent and chaste behavior" (vv. 1–2, RSV). But that wasn't the time to say anything.

Multiplying my prayers for her, I entrusted Jan to God and kept my "hands-off" policy going those fourteen months. Without mentioning to anybody what I was doing, I silently stayed in God's Word, wept and prayed, "Lord, don't change Chris, don't change Jan, don't change my other children, don't change the people in my church, don't change anybody else—but, Lord, change Evelyn."

Now eight years later, I have just had the shock of my life. A doctor's wife from our church greeted me one Sunday morning and said, "I was chatting with your Jan at our Christian Medical Society's retreat, and she told me that she gets her philosophy of life from her mother." And it was Jan herself who had said to me just days before that, "Mother, your next book has to be, must be, *Lord, Change Me.*"

But the most surprising and thrilling thing to come out of those fourteen agonizing months of keeping my mouth closed and letting God change me was a birthday card the next year from my Jan. It was signed: "To my mother—who says so much in her silence."

I had learned the first step in becoming more Christ-like—*admitting* that I was the one who needed changing while in silence *living* my life before others.

The struggle paid off in many ways, but one of the most gratifying was when Nancy, our middle child, came home from her part-time job four years later, burst into the living room and said, "Mother, I found you in the Bible! I was just reading my *Living Bible* and found you in Titus 2:7." Tears came to my eyes as she read it to me. "And here you yourself must be an example to them of good deeds of every kind. Let everything you do reflect your love of the truth and the fact that you are in dead earnest about it."

I cried in my heart, "O God, have I really *lived* in front of Nancy an 'example ... of good deeds ... love of truth ... and ... in dead earnest'? Are there really those who are being won, not with my words but by observing me?"

SECTION II

How Do I Change?

2

Changed—By the Lord Through His Word

Jord, I want to change. But how do I discover *Your* 'chaste and reverent' behavior in 1 Peter 3:1–2? Especially since I've been trying so hard for so long? Is there more, Lord? How should I go about becoming what You want me to be now?"

LET HIM ASK GOD

When I asked God these questions, He showed me that *He* gives answers. All I needed to do was ask. He has promised "If any of you lack wisdom, let him ask of God, that giveth to all men liberally, and upbraideth not; and it shall be given him" (James 1:5). One definition of wisdom is "that endowment of heart and mind which is needed for the right *conduct of life*." Wisdom is not just philosophic speculation or intellectual knowledge, but a practical, applied lifestyle. It is not only knowing something in your head, but applying it to your life so that it becomes a part of you.

IF ANY LACK WISDOM

A few years before God had taught me the *process* of seeking wisdom from His Word. I had been given my first denominational assignment—to bring four messages to women's and girls' work directors from our eighteen districts in the United States and Canada on the theme, "God's Word for a New Age." I was to prove that the Bible was an adequate guide for this new age—an age of exploding knowledge, with technical libraries becoming obsolete every six months, and with a whole new world being conquered in outer space.

Trying to come up with the material for my messages, I drew a blank month after month. Finally I panicked, realizing I had only two months left to find a solution to this mind-boggling challenge. So, at 5:30 one morning, I sought my green chair "prayer closet," fell on my knees, and begged God to give me the answer. I prayed and pleaded for over an hour—but no answer came. In desperation I reached for my Bible, opened it to where I was reading devotionally, and started to read Psalm 25.

Suddenly one little four-letter word in the fifth verse almost jumped off the page at me. It seemed to be in very black bold type. W-A-I-T. "Lead me in Thy truth, and teach me; for thou art the God of my salvation; on Thee do I *wait* all the day."

"O Lord," I cried, "I'll take You at Your Word. I'll trust You. I won't read any books on the subject. I'll just stay in *Your* Book and let You tell me what I should teach those women."

Then every day for the next six weeks I read the Scriptures, not just consecutively in one book, but at random. And each time God stopped me (as He had at the word *wait*), I would jot down the specific thought on a separate piece of paper. When I finished this process during our vacation at the cottage on Lake Michigan that summer, God had a surprise for me. I looked at the hopeless pile of random notes and announced to the family that I needed to use the dining room table for a while to divide these into some semblance of order.

As I read through these disconnected, scattered thoughts gleaned from my Bible reading, I realized that they were logically dividing themselves into four specific subjects. And I no longer had one large pile but four smaller piles of paper. With mounting enthusiasm and curiosity, I reread each grouping and discovered that these random notes fell into a natural outline form. (They reminded me of my college freshman English class where we learned to make notations from our research on index cards.) In almost a state of shock I, who had always thought of myself as the "commentary kid," looked at the four piles of notes in outline form for the four messages which would prove that God's Word is an adequate guide for our sophisticated, proud minds. Wow! The Bible was alive—sufficient for our new age!

The process of obtaining wisdom from God was indelibly impressed on my mind. For six weeks He had been carefully guiding and directing my "random" reading, speaking specifically to the subject through scattered Scriptures.

WHO GIVETH TO "ALL" MEN LIBERALLY

God had another surprise for me in this process of seeking wisdom from His Word. After giving these four messages at the Regional Chairmen's Conference in Chicago and sharing them at a retreat in the foothills of Mount Rainier in Washington, I taught them at the annual fall "Learning for Serving" seminar at our church. Soon afterward a visiting college president was our guest speaker on a Sunday morning.

After the service my phone began to ring. "Did you recognize your outline this morning, Evelyn?"

"That was not *my* outline," I assured the caller. "I know that man never heard a word I ever taught. That was *his* outline, not mine."

God had taught both of us the same truths from His Word! I don't know the method God used to give our guest speaker his message, but it overwhelmed me that identical instructions had been given to both of us.

The following January I kept my radio tuned to Moody Bible

Institute's annual Founder's Week broadcasts while doing my housework. Day after day I listened in stunned silence as two nationally known speakers used the same points and illustrations God had given me in that random reading the previous summer for my "God's Word for a New Age" project. Finally I pressed the "off" buttons of the washer and dryer, ran into the dining room and dropped my head in my arms on the table. "O God," I sobbed, "You gave *me* the same information out of Your Word that You gave those two great men of God with earned Ph.D. degrees! *Me*—a nobody!"

READ UNTIL

It was two years later that God offered me the new project of "Lord, change me," which originated with my oldest daughter's criticism. This time I was to let God change me through His Word while I kept my philosophy to myself. Most mothers go through a time of deep introspection when their children leave the nest. Now I had joined their ranks. I too reevaluated myself—soon to be out of a job just as I was becoming experienced at being a mother.

I set out in earnest using the process God had taught me, allowing Him to tell me *how* He wanted me to change. Staying in the Scripture for instruction, I would read only *until* He spoke. Then I would stop to pray about what He had said, analyze His reason for stopping me at that particular point, discover the need He knew I had, and then determine what I could do to change. I underlined hundreds of verses during those fourteen months, but I'll share here only a few that were the most meaningful to me.

As I read in the Psalms day by day, God gave me the *source* of wisdom that would effect changes in my life. First, He gave me Psalm 1:2, "But his delight is in the law of the Lord; and in His law doth he meditate day and night." In the margin of my Bible by that verse I wrote: "twenty-four hours" and "all undergraduates, no alumni." I was to meditate in His law day and night, and not consider myself as having graduated from God's school of learning and changing. There was still more for me to learn.

How I was to approach this process was shown to me in Psalm 25: "The meek will He guide in judgment; and the meek will He teach His way" (v. 9), and "What man is he that feareth the Lord? Him shall He teach in the way that He shall choose" (v.12). Coming to God humbly and meekly, admitting that *I* needed to be changed, was a new, emerging thought to me in those days.

Then underlined heavily in my Bible was *the promise of authoritative direction from God* for me in Psalm 32:8: "I will instruct thee and teach thee in the way which thou shalt go; I will guide thee with Mine eye." There was no question about it, God was going to instruct me and He was going to guide me in my quest for instruction as to *how* I was to change.

As God spoke to me forcefully out of the 139th Psalm, the idea of Scripture being profitable for reproof (2 Tim. 3:16) became evident. "Search me, O God, and know my heart; try me, and know my thoughts; and see if there be any wicked way in me, and lead me in the way everlasting" (Ps. 139:23–24). God had to show me through His Word what displeased Him and what needed to be changed in me. In the margin I penciled, "Prayer: 'Lord, change me.'"

Then, I read until God spoke from the Book of Proverbs. During those fourteen months, He gave me much instruction about obtaining wisdom: "Yea, if thou *criest* after knowledge, and liftest up thy voice for understanding; if thou *seekest* her as silver, and *searchest* for her as for hid treasures; then shalt thou understand the fear of the Lord, and find the knowledge of God. For the Lord, giveth wisdom; out of His mouth cometh knowledge and understanding" (Proverbs 2:3–6, italics mine). Once again God was impressing upon me the truth that "the fear of the Lord is the beginning of wisdom" (9:10). And that wisdom was to be found in His Word.

TRANSFORMED—BY THE RENEWING OF YOUR MIND

Some specific points on how I could change began emerging during those fourteen months as I searched the Scriptures. I remember rising early in the morning in a Fort Lauderdale condominium, struggling with what God meant when He had given me Romans 12:2 the month before: "But be not conformed to this world: but be ye transformed by the renewing of your mind, that ye may prove what is that good, and acceptable, and perfect will of God."

The next December I wrote in the margin of my Bible, "Transformed—same word as Christ's transfiguration." Did God want me changed as dramatically as Christ was on the Mount of Transfiguration when His face shone as the sun and His raiment was white as the light? Then I wrote, "Changed—from worm to butterfly." I almost felt like the surprised worm I had seen on a poster. Watching a butterfly soar overhead, the worm was saying, "Who, *me* change?" Then I wrote in the margin of my Bible beside Romans 12:2, "Pronouns—does God want *me*?" The pronouns were so very, very personal. I circled them. No mistaking it—God wasn't talking to my husband, my children—but to me. Then the abrupt note in my Bible said, "Spiritual maturity—period." Yes, that's what all that changing was about—to be mature in Him. Like Him. Proving what is His good and acceptable and perfect will—for me.

God also told me how I *didn't* have to change. Although I felt inner compulsion to give up my teaching and speaking after I had told God I would that previous June, it was such a thrill to get this confirmation directly from Him. As I was reading in Ephesians 6, I blinked in surprise. Then tears of relief swelled in my eyes as He stopped me at verses 19 and 20: "And for me, that utterance may be given unto me, that I may open my mouth boldly, to make known the mystery of the Gospel, for which I am an ambassador in bonds; that therein I may speak boldly, as I ought to speak." This was one of the greatest things God taught me those fourteen months. He told me to continue speaking and teaching even though I was willing to give it all up if it was going to hurt my husband. My final affirmation to this came the next fall from my husband himself when he said to me, "Honey, I'm your greatest fan."

God continued to show me how to change. In February, I read Galatians 2:20: "I am crucified with Christ; nevertheless I live; yet not I, but Christ liveth in me; and the life which I now live in the flesh I live by the faith of the Son of God, who loved me and gave Himself for me." Then, in my Bible, I wrote, "Ego moves to the side—Christ center of me." Then *how* to change was becoming obvious. I was to let Christ live in me, transforming me into the likeness of Himself.

There were many specific instructions, but Philippians 2:3, with the notation, "Humility—April," was so meaningful to me at that time: "Let nothing be done through strife or vainglory; but in lowliness of mind let each esteem others better than themselves."

God even showed me some affirmation of the learning in silence through my 11-year-old Kurt as we were reading together that January. "Isn't it amazing how much you can learn when you don't argue?" he commented on Philippians 2:14: "Do all things without murmurings and disputings." Renewing my mind!

God seemed to reassure me through one verse of Scripture in my struggle to become changed, more Christ-like. In February I had a heavy speaking schedule and was utterly exhausted at a retreat in Mount Hermon, California. I fervently prayed for God to change me before the Saturday night banquet. Two days later, after an almost miraculous rejuvenation for the banquet, I marked this in my Bible: "Being confident of this very thing, that He who hath begun a good work in you will perform it until the day of Jesus Christ" (Phil. 1:6).

That same February, a verse I would only be able to understand later prompted me to write "me" in the margin beside it. Like Paul, would I be a more effective servant of Jesus after this? Would my ministry for Christ be more effective because of the experiences of these fourteen months? "But I would ye should understand, brethren, that the things which happened unto *me* have fallen out rather unto the furtherance of the Gospel" (Phil. 1:12).

PRECEPT UPON PRECEPT

Then God gave some more specific instructions about His method of teaching me those fourteen months. On March 23, 1969, He showed me emphatically that He was the Teacher. "But the anointing which ye have received of Him abideth in you, and ye need not that any man teach you but as the same anointing teacheth you of all things, and is truth, and is no lie, and even as it hath taught you, ye shall abide in Him" (1 John 2:27). "Whom shall He teach knowledge? And whom shall He make to understand doctrine? Them that are weaned from the milk, and drawn from the breasts. *For precept must be upon precept*, precept upon precept; line upon line, line upon line; here a little, and there a little" (Isa. 28:9–10, italics mine).

That was it. Through hundreds of verses God spoke directly to me during that time. He had piled precept upon precept and line upon line, showing me what needed to be changed, and how to depend completely upon Him for wisdom to change. This maturing was for those who were weaned from milk, those who were growing up—by the renewing of the mind!

AND UPBRAIDETH NOT

Never once in those fourteen months did God scold me for asking for more wisdom. Over and over again He reassured me that He wanted to give me all the wisdom I needed. The gift of wisdom is the only gift promised to *all* who ask for it. The other gifts are given by the three Persons of the Trinity as They please to distribute them.

In 1 Corinthians 12:8–11 we read that the Holy Spirit divides gifts to every man as He wills. Romans 12:3–6 shows us that "God hath dealt to every man the measure of faith … having then gifts differing according to the grace that is given to us." Then, in Ephesians 4:7 and 11, we read, "But unto every one of us is given grace according to the measure of the gift of Christ … and He gave some, apostles; some, prophets; and some, evangelists; and some, pastors and teachers." Thus Christ, too gave people differing gifts to the churches as He desired. But the gift of wisdom is different. All believers can ask for and receive the precious gift of wisdom for making changes in their lives. They are given a renewed mind to know the perfect will of God.

CHANGED—THROUGH MY SPIRITUAL DIARY

But receiving wisdom for my life from His Word has not been confined to those fourteen months. Recently I did a project in preparation for an assigned retreat theme of "God's Living Word." To prove to myself—and those at the retreat—that the Bible had been alive in my own life, I dug out the three Bibles I had used since high school and systematically and laboriously recorded in three columns (one for each Bible) the most significant underlined, and usually dated, Scriptures. As I pored over these three Bibles for a month I had a surprise. I could tell from the passage I had underlined whether I had been in victory or defeat, joy or depression, death, birth, surgery, illness, open doors, challenge, or closed doors. And as the evidence piled up, I slowly began to realize that God had *always* given *specific answers for specific needs at specific times.*

As column after column on page after page filled up on the legal pad I was using, something overwhelmingly significant came into focus. I had in three Bibles a *spiritual diary of my life* from the time I was eighteen! For all of those years God had been instructing me specifically out of His Word. The process that came into focus as "Lord, change me" that June actually had been an unrecognized goal of my life since I had graduated from high school in 1940.

May I share a few of the verses that are most precious to me, selected from the thousands underlined and usually dated in those three Bibles?

*   *   *

At our first pastorate in the fall of 1953 God spoke definitely to me the day the doctors told us our baby, Judy, could not live. I remember taking her to the hospital, coming home with aching, empty arms and a horrible rebellion in my heart—stubbornly hanging on to my right to keep her. I struggled alone in my bedroom for hours over a statement our former pastor had made, "God must love Harold and Evelyn a lot to give them all that sorrow." As I thought about the Scripture he was referring to in Hebrew 12:6, "For whom the Lord loveth He chasteneth," I became more and more angry at him for saying such a terrible thing.

But as I fought with God in my solitude, He seemed to be saying to me, "Read on." So I opened my Bible and read to Hebrews 12:10 where it says that our earthly fathers "chastened us after their own pleasure; but He [God] for our profit." God seemed to be whispering to me that, if I was going to be a pastor's wife, I would have to understand some of these things. I would need compassion when I was called upon to stand beside a crib in a hospital or by a little casket. I could only be all He wanted me to be as a pastor's wife as I experienced this chastening. Then verse 11 explained it all: "Now no chastening for the present seemeth to be joyous, but grievous; nevertheless *afterward* it yieldeth the peaceable fruit of righteousness unto them which *are exercised thereby*" (italics mine).

I felt my stubborn will go limp within me—at the same moment my tense, rebelling body crumpled on the bed beside which I was kneeling. I had surrendered to His will, whatever that might be. And at that point God changed me. My battle was over. My rebellion ceased. From that point on there was no struggle, although there were two more months of watching Judy slowly burn out. I was filled with grief on the day she died—but there was no rebellion. He had prepared me for those difficult days—but even more so for all the years ahead. God had changed me by *exercising* me with chastening. But it was all for my profit—so that I could be a "partaker of His holiness." And that "peaceable fruit of righteousness" did come at last.

*   *   *

I was quite shaken when a pastor's wife accused me publicly of leaving out a theologically important point in a message. Checking the tape of the message later, and finding that I really *had* said it, didn't ease the embarrassment. But God had the answer for me. The next morning as I read Psalm 19 one word stood out in the 14th verse—"Thy." "Let the words of my mouth, and the meditation of my heart, be acceptable in Thy sight, O Lord, my strength, and my Redeemer."

In the margin of the Bible I wrote, "In *Thy* sight, not in people's sight." And then I prayed, asking the Lord to remove all the negative thoughts I had had the night before. I asked Him to forgive me and "make EVERY thought and ALL my words acceptable to YOU, LORD!" Immediately I sensed His affirmation, His OK on that message. The desire to defend my innocence melted. God had changed me!

*   *   *

It was pouring rain as I started for an out-of-state retreat in April. Three miles from home a truck, a compact car, and Evelyn stopped for a red light, but the car behind me didn't. Crunch. And all four vehicles accordioned into one. I recovered from the jolt to my back but evidently not from the jolt to my nervous system, for as I drove during the following week I kept my eyes as much on the rearview mirror as I did on the road ahead of me! And the next weekend I was to drive to a northern Minnesota retreat. I couldn't. I felt nothing but apprehension and fear at the possibility of being hit from behind. And the theme for the retreat was to be J-O-Y! But just before I was to drive to the retreat, God gave the answer as I was reading in the Psalms. A smile spread over my face as I read: "But let all those who put their trust in Thee rejoice; let them ever shout for *joy*, because Thou defendest them; let them also that love Thy name be joyful in Thee" (Ps. 5:11). Immediately I saw my problem—failing to trust Him! At that moment He exchanged my fear for His—yes, literally—His joy. The apprehension disappeared, and I drove, a changed woman, to that J-O-Y retreat, really experiencing what I was to preach.

My spiritual barometer for years has been 1 John 1:4: "These things [are written] that your joy may be full." I can always measure the amount of time I'm spending in the Scriptures by how much joy (not superficial happiness, but deep down abiding joy) I have. When I find a lack of joy in my life, the first thing I check is how much time I'm spending in God's Word!

*   *   *

I'll never forget speaking at a convention where our schedule included breakfast, morning coffee and rolls, lunch, afternoon coffee and rolls, dinner, evening snack with sweet rolls! I had a badly sprained ankle at the time and was forced to go to my room and elevate it several times during each day. My car driver and I took that time to read the Bible together, practicing the "until He speaks" process.

One afternoon Luke 4:4 took on a completely new meaning: "Man [or woman] shall not live by bread alone, but by every word of God."

I actually found myself thanking God for my sprained ankle so I could exchange some of the sweet rolls for the Bread of Life. I wrote in the margin of my Bible: "Plenty of time for coffee and rolls, but not enough time for God's Word alone."

*   *   *

I'm convinced that God has a sense of humor. Our church experienced a great moving of God, and every Sunday for four months I had the privilege of praying with at least one, and frequently with many, who came to find Christ as their Savior. It was exciting. But suddenly I had pain in my middle and was hospitalized for tests. A "No Water" sign was hung on the end of my bed, and by early morning the real or imagined desperation for water had set in. In my discomfort I prayed, "God, please give me something to read in my Bible that's just for me, right now." And Psalm 63 popped into my head, although I didn't have the foggiest idea what it was about. I grabbed my Bible, turned to the psalm, and read: "Oh, God, Thou are my God; early will I seek Thee." So far so good. It was 5:30 in the morning.

As I read on in that first verse, I cried, "Lord, is this a joke?" "My soul thirsteth for Thee, my flesh longeth for Thee in a dry and thirsty land, where no water is."

Then I saw in verse 2 what God was really trying to say to me: "To see Thy power and Thy glory, so as I have seen Thee in the sanctuary." God showed me that my real problem was not the lack of water, but in not wanting to miss seeing Him move in the sanctuary. My real rebellion was being put on a shelf in the midst of the action!

*   *   *

When the tests were over I remembered smiling bravely as my doctor told me that I would have to have surgery right away. I nodded and smiled until he disappeared out the door, and then burst into tears. Reaching for my Bible, I prayed, "Oh, God, give me something for *right now!*" Immediately Romans 12:1 flashed into my mind, and I turned to it, "I beseech you, therefore brethren, by the mercies of God, that ye present your bodies a living sacrifice, holy acceptable unto God, which is your reasonable service."

Now I had His answer. I had given Him so completely my spirit—my mind, my emotions, my energy. All that I was, I thought. But *I had never given Him my body!*

Surgery and days of recuperation came and went, but I was still kicking at being left on a shelf when so much was going on in "the sanctuary." Not until the next Sunday when I tuned into a pastor friend's radio program did I obey God's instruction to me. I was still kicking because *my* body was in a hospital bed instead of at church that morning. But a little poem he read, "Gaining Through Losing," struck a responsive chord, and I gave God my body—once and for all. (I knew the verb tense of "gave" in Romans 12:1 was a once-for-all and not continuous action.)

Gradually my attitude toward my health changed. Illness didn't disappear completely (although its diminishing frequency has been rather amazing), but my *attitude* toward it changed. I relaxed. I felt somewhat like the pastor who called his banker saying *our* car is in the ditch. Through the years I have learned to say, "God, *our* body is sick."

God changed me from an overprotective guardian of my body to one who entrusts that body to Him. What a great way to live! No friction, no hassle. Whenever I don't feel well, I just say, "Lord, if You want me to be well enough to do the job for You that's coming up, thank You. But if not, just teach me what You have for me to learn while I'm on a shelf." This obedience to His specific instruction has done more than anything else in my life to take the pressure off and change my whole outlook on life.

*   *   *

One of the favorite things we do during our vacation in Michigan around August 12 is to lie on the beach at midnight and watch the fantastic display of shooting stars. The summer our Kurt was seven I read an article in *Reader's Digest* about a father who got his seven-year-old boy up in the middle of the night to see the shooting stars because, he reasoned, there were some things more important than sleep. So, when the exhibition was at its peak, we decided it was time for Kurt to join the rest of the family on the beach. The excitement and the "oh's" and "ah's" mounted with each display of God's celestial fireworks.

But the real excitement came the next morning when, as a family, we read at the breakfast table Psalm 33, and especially the fifth to ninth verses: "The earth is full of the goodness of the Lord. By the word of the Lord were the heavens made; and all the host of them by the breath of His mouth. ... Let all the inhabitants of the world stand in awe of Him, for He spake, and it was done." I found myself not only excited over an astronomical wonder, but changed into a mother awed at God's timing and selection of our daily reading—overawed that He wanted to tell us that He only had to speak and all this was done!

*   *   *

The beach at Lake Michigan is also my favorite place to read God's Word and let Him speak to me. Every day while we are on vacation I rise early and, weather permitting, take my Bible down to the edge of the lake and read until He speaks. One morning I read such a great psalm about our God that I found myself skipping down the beach instead of doing my usual hiking. God had changed an ordinary, run-of-the-mill vacation day into one of exhilaration and exploding joy, joy that could not be contained in ordinary steps. The thrill that sent my body soaring like the eagle's burst out in impromptu songs of praise as I adored Him for who He is and praised Him for what He is. Changed by a psalm? Yes, changed!

Thirty-six years of underlining answers for actual situations have proven to me that the Bible truly is a *living* Book. "For the Word of God is living and active," Hebrews 4:12 (NASB) tells us. Yes, it is alive. It has answers in the midst of our knowledge explosion today—or tomorrow— on this planet and in outer space. And precept upon precept as I let it renew my mind and my attitudes, I am changed. Changed into what is His perfect will for me to be.

TREASURE

I packed those three Bibles in my tote bag to show at that retreat where I was to speak on "God's Living Word." As I headed for the plane in Minneapolis, the security guard started systematically to check my carry-on luggage. When he pulled out the first Bible he gave me a "that's-a-nice-lady" smile. The second one produced a puzzled expression on his face. But, at finding the third, he was sure I had hidden something valuable in those Bibles, and proceeded to search each one diligently. He even held one up by its binding and shook it vigorously.

That guard never discovered the treasure I had hidden in those three Bibles. The omniscient Lord Jesus Christ, "in whom are hid all the treasures of wisdom and knowledge" (Col. 2:3), had given it to me. Underlined and marked on those pages was all the direction I had needed for a "chaste and reverent" lifestyle since I was eighteen years old. Line upon line, precept upon precept, God had taught me how to change.

When I have needed direction for my life, had He ever left me groping in the dark, trying to find my way? Oh, no! He had given me His Word as a "lamp unto my feet, and a light unto my path" (Ps. 119:105). And, as I have obeyed His instructions, He has *changed me*, step by step, into the person He wants me to be.

3

Changed—For Others Too

*T*hose fourteen months marched silently along with God continuing His rebuking, refining, enlightening, changing. I was aware of each step, but still had not thought of it as anything more than a process for me.

But suddenly the months of searching Scripture "without a word" were over. The "Lord, change me" gestation period which started in June 1968 came to an end and the hidden theme was born. What had been a very private experience in my own life erupted, unplanned, at a Minnesota Baptist Women's Retreat at Big Trout Lake; Minnesota. Unannounced, it became a principle to be shared with others.

"Did the theme of this retreat change?" asked a committee member.

"To what do you think it changed?" I asked.

"I think it changed to 'Lord, Change Me.'"

"I think it did too. But I didn't change it. God did."

No, I hadn't changed the theme. I had diligently prepared my messages on the theme those 800 women had chosen for their retreat—but God had other ideas.

Just before I started to speak on the first night of that retreat, someone slipped a note to me: "Please come to our cabin. We have a problem." I tucked the note in my Bible, promising myself to see about the need after the service.

While I spoke that night, one illustration from a previous women's retreat was to trigger the change of the theme. I told these Minnesota women how right after I had found such exciting answers when I had read only the Bible, I decided to try the wait process on the 400 women attending a retreat in the foothills of Mount Rainier in Washington. Having no idea of what God was going to say to them, I sent those women out to read Colossians 3 by themselves. I had instructed them to read only *until* God spoke, and then to stop and pray about what He was saying to them.

In addition to speaking at that Mount Rainier retreat, I told them, I had also served as counselor. A steady stream of women came to me for advice—talking to me while I brushed my teeth, and even shouting over the shower curtain. I knew I didn't have professional answers for those women, so every time one came to me I listened to her problem and then asked the question: "And where did God stop you in your reading of Colossians 3 today?" I felt I was on safe ground asking that question.

And do you know what happened? *In every instance* the Lord stopped *each one of them* at the answer to her problem. I didn't have to offer a single solution, because the Lord did. In fact, on Saturday night the retreat committee said to me, "God is doing such a great thing, let's not structure the Sunday morning service. Let's just ask the women to share what God has been saying to them out of the Scripture."

That Sunday morning for one-and-a-half hours the women kept popping up like popcorn sharing what God had said. I was so overwhelmed that I finally asked them all to jot down on a piece of paper what God showed them when He stopped them in Colossians 3. I went home to Minnesota with a large manila envelope bulging with specific answers—not from me but from God.

I told the Minnesota women that as I was hurriedly throwing things into my suitcase to catch a plane for Minneapolis, a very angry and distraught woman burst into my room. I explained that I really didn't have time to talk with her, but she told me to keep packing while she talked. She trembled with anger as she ranted on about a woman she couldn't stand, a woman who was also attending the retreat. "Why," she exploded, "she actually talks and gossips about our pastor. And I won't go to prayer meeting if she's going to be there because I get so furious when she prays. Would you believe she actually prays against him right in front of him?"

As she raved on, I paused in my packing, turned to her and asked, "And where did God stop you in Colossians 3?"

"In verse 13."

"What does it say?"

"It says, 'Forebearing one another, and forgiving one another, if any man have a quarrel against any; even as Christ forgave you, so also do ye.'"

"Is that where He stopped you?" (Nod.) "How long have you been a Christian?"

"Three months."

"Did Christ forgive anything in you when you became a Christian?"

A look of shock crossed her face. Then she put her head on my shoulder and began to weep. "Oh, it's *my* fault, isn't it? I'm the one who needs to change, not her. I'm the one God needs to change." She had seen that she was to forgive others *as* He had forgiven her—forgiven her of all her past sins when she accepted Him as her Savior three months before.

I went to the airport with a wet shoulder, but left behind a woman who had learned to forgive as Christ had forgiven her—because God had shown her what was wrong with herself, not with the other woman.

That's the story I told at the Minnesota retreat before going to the cabin whose members had sent me a note just before the meeting. Though it was a warm September night, when I entered the cabin, I was sure there were icicles hanging from the ceiling. I have never felt a colder atmosphere. All the women were sitting there in sullen silence with their chins slightly jutted and arms crossed.

I soon discovered that they were all from the same small town where their church recently split. Half of them had stayed in the church and the other half had left. At home they weren't speaking to one another. But the unknowing camp registrar had put them all in the same cabin!

And there they sat—each one blaming the other. My first suggestion was that they read Colossians 3.

"No!" One lady was sitting cross-legged on her bed right beside me, holding her Bible. I asked her several times to read Colossians 3:13 for us, but she stubbornly repeated, "No, I won't."

A couple of hours passed, but I was getting nowhere. They finally agreed on one point; the problem in their town was all the fault of one man—*he* did this, and *he* did that. And if *he* hadn't done that, *we* wouldn't have done that. "Yes," they all agreed, "it is all his fault because our church broke up."

"He sounds like a pretty horrible guy, and I guess it is probably all his fault—or at least most of it is. But," I said, "do you think 1 percent of the blame might be in this room?"

"No! Uh-uh! There's nothing wrong in *this* room."

But I kept pushing the point. "Could there *possibly* be just one percent?"

Then from the far corner a woman said hesitantly, in a barely audible voice, "I think there's 1 percent over here."

Then someone else said, "I think maybe there's, ah, 10 percent here."

Finally the woman with the Bible, sitting cross-legged on her bed, looked at me and stammered, "I—I think I can read Colossians 3:13 now." And slowly she read: "Forgiving one another, if any man have a quarrel against any; even as Christ forgave you, so also do ye."

At a quarter to one in the morning, we finally ended the encounter with our arms around each other, weeping and praying. And those women prayed only one prayer, "Oh, Lord, don't change that guy back home. *Change me!*"

The next night at our campfire sharing time, the "Lord, Change Me" theme continued. Woman after woman kept saying, "I needed changing—not everybody else." One women society's president said, "Nine of my women had made reservations for this retreat, and I kept saying of each one, 'Isn't that wonderful; does *she* need it!' And then my phone started ringing, and one after another was saying that she couldn't make it. I would hang up the phone and think, 'Isn't it too bad; *she* needed it so badly.' Finally there were just four going from our church. But tonight I realize that it wasn't all the women who couldn't come who needed this retreat; *I* am the one who needed it."

Yes, I knew the theme of the retreat had changed. I had watched it change. But I hadn't changed it—God had. Thus "Lord, Change Me" for groups was launched—to be used with thousands of people, always with the same results, all over the United States and Canada.

ANOTHER SURPRISE

On the first Monday following that Minnesota retreat, God had another surprise for me in the unfolding of the "Lord, Change Me" theme.

Early in the morning our front doorbell rang and there stood a man my husband had counseled many, many times. He had been married, divorced, and remarried to the same woman. And his life was still a horrible mess. "Could I see the pastor?" he asked.

My mother-hen defense for Christ went up and I said, "It's terribly early and Chris is still asleep. Could you come a bit later?"

"I *have* to tell somebody. Could I tell you?"

Monday morning! But I said, "Wait until I turn off the washer and dryer." I returned, pulled my robe tighter around me as I sat down on the davenport and said, "OK. Tell me."

He said, "Do you know what? The most amazing thing happened to me."

And I halfheartedly countered, "Really?"

"Yup. A week ago I was driving my truck down Broadway, and I was blaming everybody for what was going on in my home—my kids, my wife, my employer. But suddenly the Lord said to me, '*You* are the one who needs to be changed, not all the rest of the people. *You* need to be changed.' As I drove I think I even closed my eyes once and prayed, 'Lord, change *me*; Lord, change *me*.'"

I sat there in amazement: *Lord, change me!*

It was all coming into focus. The "Lord, change me" concept had been given to him too. It was spreading. God was spreading it!

"I have had the most marvelous experience," he continued. "I went home, and there was that wife that I married, divorced, and remarried. We were having such a rough time. And the next morning when I woke up there she was, the same wife. But I loved her with a love I didn't know was possible. I took her in my arms and said, 'Oh, honey, how I love you.' It was just great. I loved her, and I loved the kids.

"Now, I hadn't gotten along with my dad" he continued. "We hadn't really spoken for many years. I got in the car and went out to see my old dad who had been an invalid for a long time. I went to his bedside, took his hand, and said, 'Dad, I just came here for one reason. I came here to tell you I love you.' And the tears started to trickle down his face as he took my hand and said, 'Sonny, I have waited since you were that high (measuring three feet from the floor with his hand) to hear you say that.'

"Then I went to church on Sunday morning, and there was my wife's lawyer who knew all the dirt about me. I thought I was ready to join the church that morning, but I knew that I had some unfinished business. Instead of going down front to say that I wanted to join the church, I turned around and swung over to my wife's lawyer. The two of us put our arms around each other, and stood there in the sanctuary and wept. The next person I saw was a businessman who had done me dirt—a Christian, member of our church. I got to thinking, 'I haven't been so honest with him either.' And I walked up to that man, looked him right in the eye, and stuck out my hand. We shook hands.

"Mrs. Chris, I *had* to tell somebody, because all I've been praying is 'Lord, change me.' *And all of these things have happened in my whole relationship with people—just because I prayed 'Lord,—change—me!'*"

This is the exciting part of the changing process! Relationships with people do change when we pray, "Lord, change *me*." And I now realized that God had not given this fabulous thought to me to be kept selfishly to myself—only to see myself change. But He had intended all along that it was to be shared with others whom He also wanted to change.

"WE WANT A 'LORD, CHANGE ME' RETREAT TOO"

The next morning I went to our weekly prayer meeting with my heart absolutely overflowing. I decided it was time to share "Lord, change me" with my dear women. I told them what God had been doing in my life for fourteen months, and then how the process had miraculously erupted, unplanned, at the Minnesota retreat the preceding week. Then I shared the startling story that had been told to me the morning before. When I finished, one wide-eyed member of our prayer group said, "I think we need a 'Lord, change me' retreat too."

So we planned what was to be my first women's "Lord, change me" retreat. For the next month our president and I struggled, trying to put together an agenda, but to no avail. The day before the scheduled retreat, we communicated five times trying to figure out what to do all day long, but the Lord kept telling both of us, "Just trust Me. Just trust Me."

The next morning I was a little apprehensive as the church parking lot started to fill with cars. The officers of our women's organizations were gathering to form a caravan to a cottage in Wisconsin for our first "Lord, change me" retreat. They were trusting God, and the responsibility was a bit overwhelming. Armed with nothing but our Bibles, we wended our way to our all-day retreat. As we traveled I kept praying silently, "Oh, Lord, just You—just You."

The great part of trusting the Lord is that He never lets you down. I spent the first twenty minutes of that retreat sharing my excitement over what God had done in my own life for fourteen months, the Minnesota retreat, the Monday morning visitor, and then the prayer group's request for this retreat. That was all.

From then on that day we let God be in command. I assigned a portion of Scripture, instructing them to "take this portion of Scripture, find any spot you want in this cabin, and read until God speaks to you. Read *only until* He speaks. Don't read any more. If you read on after He speaks, you'll get confused, not knowing what you should pray about. Then, ask God *why* He stopped you at that point, *what needs changing* in your life, and then *what He wants you to do* about it. Be sure to listen as He gently brings answers to your mind. God's speaking to you in the Scripture may be only a little nudge, or you may think some words are popping out in bold print."

Then we prayed a simple prayer. "Lord, remove all our preconceived ideas about this portion of Scripture. We want You to tell us *afresh* what You want changed in us *today*." I asked for complete silence, explaining that it is impossible for God to speak to us if we are chattering, discussing, and talking to each other. So, a slightly bewildered but willing group sought their private spots with the Lord and began reading.

I sat in the living room wondering what would happen. For almost two years these women had been experimenting with what happened when they prayed, learning to pray first and plan afterward, and then to bear one another's burdens in prayer. Did God have another step for *them* too?

At 11 o'clock we came back together and formed a large circle of prayer on our knees in the living room. Then the miracle began. We had agreed not to talk to each other, but we prayed aloud to God about where He has stopped us in the Scripture portion. I can't find any word to describe what happened next but "revival." Those women wept and prayed on their faces before God, confessing what He had told them was wrong in their lives.

"Lord, I'm sorry. Forgive me. Lord, change me," they all prayed. He had put His finger on specific needs in their lives—all of them out of the same portion of Scripture. Tears were abundant, including those in my own eyes as I listened in amazement at the way God had been faithful to His "just trust Me" promise the day before.

Through the years I have never ceased to be astounded at this process as I've led thousands to read *until* God speaks. He who knows the thoughts and intents of every heart digs deeply into the hidden recesses to search out sins and shortcomings we are often not aware of. And He does it in response to our sincere prayer to be shown what *He* wants to change in us.

During lunch we continued our silence so that we could keep listening to God. As the leader, I thanked our hostess in advance for the noodle casserole, and once again felt a slight anxiety in my heart about the unaccustomed silence. But I was put at ease at our very next session when one woman reported, "It was embarrassing when I first sat down. I sat there eating my hot dish, and I didn't know what to do. And then all at once God started to talk to me about the thing in my life He had convicted me of that morning. He penetrated deeper and deeper. I wasn't aware that there was anyone else at the table because I was alone with God, and He was speaking to me." Most of the women agreed that this was their experience during that time of silence.

In the afternoon of our first "Lord, change me" retreat, we concentrated on what God wanted to change in our circles and women's church meetings. Assigning another portion of Scripture, we prayed asking God to show us specific things He knew needed changing in our organizations. After listening to God speak to us from Romans 12, we prayed together as officers of our individual circles about what God had shown us. Then, just before our day apart was over, we gathered and asked our secretary to take notes as we shared all the things God had said needed to be changed in our circles. Those ladies bombarded our secretary with the ideas God gave them:

Circle officers should meet before each meeting to ask God's guidance.

Pray about purpose of our circles.

Do what *God* says to do.

Make inactive members feel wanted.

We must meet the needs of *all* ages in our circles.

Have a "Lord, change me" night in our circles next month.

Show compassion and love by doing kind deeds, invite, offer to pick up.

Postcards to tell them they were missed.

Help and teach, don't push.

Everyone has a talent; use it to make all feel needed.

I was so astounded at God's advice that when I got home I reread that portion wondering how He ever found some of those things in that passage to tell those ladies.

But the climax came when our shocked president looked in amazement at the women and then at a list she had dug out of her notebook. "Ladies, I have here a whole list of things I thought needed changing in your circles, and gripes from people who have wanted to see this or that changed; but I don't have to read it to you. God has told one or the other of you every single problem I have listed here and what should be done about it. I don't have to say a word!"

Yes, God had another exciting experiment for the "what-happens-when-women-pray" ladies of our church. And He had indelibly written on my heart how He can speak to specific personal and organizational needs without the president or pastor's wife saying a word. "If any of you lack wisdom, let him ask of God, who giveth to all men liberally" (James 1:5).

A REALITY: 2 TIMOTHY 3:16

"All Scripture is given by inspiration of God, and is profitable for doctrine, for reproof, for correction, for instruction in righteousness" (2 Tim. 3:16)

Sometimes God stops us on something He wants changed in our beliefs only—in our doctrine. But most of the time He deals with the three other facets in this verse—what He wants changed *in our actions*.

God frequently uses this method of reading until He speaks for *reproof*—the process of exposing and convicting of things He is dissatisfied with in our lives. One woman kept coming to me at a retreat asking me what to do about her husband who was not assuming his role as spiritual head of the house. I used every scriptural approach I knew, but nothing seemed to provide the answer.

When I arrived home, I received a letter from her. She wrote, "Dear Evelyn: Please forgive me. I wasn't honest with you, so you couldn't possibly have known my real problem and given me the right answer. But when I was reading our assigned chapter, God stopped me on my real problem—a little three-letter word 'own.' I am the secretary for a pastor. He's my ideal. I get all of my spiritual insights and help from him. At the retreat God showed me while reading His Word that I should 'be in subjection to my *own* husband.'"

About six months later I was visiting in her church, and after the service I heard, "Here's Larry, Evelyn. Here's Larry, Evelyn."

"Who's Larry?" I wondered.

I looked up to see this woman with her *own* husband in tow, happily beaming at me. Then I remembered—he was her *own* husband, the now obvious spiritual head of her house.

A young convert had been invited to one of my retreats to be our Sunday School speaker. It was obvious from the beginning that she had come to show us that she had arrived spiritually and we had not. But at our Saturday night testimony meeting around the campfire, she stood up and said, "I would give anything if any one of you would take that Sunday School hour tomorrow morning. I came here feeling so superior to you. But I took my Bible this afternoon as I was told and read God's Word. And," she said as her voice choked, "He stopped me on the word 'humbleness,' and I know now that I came here because of pride. God had to show me that He wanted me to be humble and have humility. All I have is pride in my own self-attainment. Please will one of you take that Sunday School hour tomorrow morning?"

I was really shocked at a not-so-typical example of God stopping at specific problems at one retreat. During our sharing time there was absolute silence as four pastors' wives stood up at different times and said, "My husband left the pastorate (each said some time within the last twelve months), and God has told me out of His Word today that it was all *my* fault." How God reaches down and puts His finger of reproof right on the word or words we need.

It is interesting to watch God use *restoration to an upright state* from 2 Timothy 3:16 at our retreats. One Friday night at a weekend retreat the wife of a seminary student said her retreat roommate was so angry that she was just about kicking the furniture because her seminary-student husband had received a call to a place to which she did not want to go. She asked me if I would see if I could calm her down and counsel with her.

"Let's wait until we read in God's Word tomorrow, and see what He says to her," I suggested, and she agreed.

At sharing time the next day so many in the group were stating that God stopped them in Galatians 5 concerning the leading of the Holy Spirit, that I finally said, "Everybody whom the Lord stopped on the Holy Spirit's leading and their following, please stand up." To my surprise, the angry wife of the night before stood up (with nearly half the whole audience—another surprise). As she was telling us all about it, I leaned over the pulpit and asked, "Does that mean to so-and-so city too?"

"Yes, it does," she beamed back at me.

I didn't have to say a word. God had put His finger on her problem, and she had said in her heart that she was willing to be changed into a willing follower of the Holy Spirit's leading.

A thank-you letter after a retreat said it so well, and only God could have know the need in her heart.

"Dear Evelyn: I'm so thankful for the Key '73 retreat. I learned what it means to have real joy! You see, I was raised in a Christian home, and I knew everything a Christian should do and be. I had it all in my head. But I found Him in my heart. God changed me that day, and I am so thankful. What impressed me was when you sent us out, alone, and without speaking, to read until He spoke to us."

Another note recorded the place God stopped one woman: "Galatians 6:2. 'Bear ye one another's burdens'—and the name of a specific person came to me immediately. Praise the Lord for His *living* Word."

Instruction in righteousness from God was evident in this note:

"Dear Evelyn: There wasn't time to share publicly, but my husband and I have considered adopting a child and adding to our family since we have the room and the money. ... I wasn't sure if it was God's will or just our do-gooder thoughts. I now know that God thinks I can and should do this. James 1:27, 'The Christian who is pure and without fault, from God the Father's point of view, is the one who takes care of orphans and widows, and who remains true to the Lord'" (TLB).

100 PERCENT OF US?

Every fall our church had kick-off for our Christian education administrators and paid staff who were to decide on the direction of their ministries for the coming year. In September, I was asked to conduct a "Lord, change me" retreat for one of them. All the C.E. board members, departmental superintendents, the general Sunday School superintendents, staff, and pastors were there. I briefly explained the process of reading until God spoke to them and assigned Galatians 5:1—6:10, then sent them off alone to read.

When we came back together we knelt to share in prayer what God had told each of us. Something astounding began to emerge: person after person prayed about God stopping him or her on some thought concerning the importance of the Holy Spirit's leading in the Christian education activities in our church. It soon became evident that God had stopped every single administrator and staff person on the same principle—let the Holy Spirit lead. My pastor husband and our assistant pastor, Gary Smalley, were kneeling side by side. When the pattern took shape, including where God had stopped them also, they both put their heads in their hands and wept!

Even more amazing than the fact that God speaks to all individually is that He speaks to many collectively about the same thing. Every time I assign this portion in Galatians, never fewer than 50 percent and up to 100 percent of the participants are stopped on the passage dealing with the Holy Spirit's leading. And this always is absolutely without any instruction as to what they are to look for or expect from God. Whenever this happens, I feel a sense of holy awe sweeping over me. God's *instruction in righteousness*—showing us the direction He wants us to go!

WRITE GOD A LETTER

Frequently at our retreats, after God has spoken to us through His Word, we write Him a letter. We tell Him what we will change in our lives because of what He has pointed out to us. After having each one seal his letter to God in a self-addressed envelope, I collect the letters and keep them for about a month. Then I put them in the mail so the writer can check up on herself to see if she really *did change*—or if she forgot and went on in the same old condition.

I always "read until" with the others at retreats, and here is one letter I wrote:

"Dear God: You told me that I am hung up on not really accepting 'that person' back into the fellowship of the beloved, and that I am to restore that person who was overtaken in a fault—lest I, Evelyn, should be tempted like that—even though I don't think that is one of my weaknesses. I will restore that person in every possible way. Lord, open doors, make me comfortable around that person again."

The very next day God honored my prayer, and arranged a surprise breakfast meeting. I keep that letter as a constant reminder of how *I* had to change in my attitude toward one who had slipped—of how God had told *me* to change and I had obeyed.

The changes come, however, not when God speaks but when we *obey* what He has told us. We are changed only when we *apply* to our lives what He has said.

A pastor and his wife were chatting with me at a conference last summer. She said, "After our 'Lord, change me' retreat, Evelyn, I went home and practiced letting the Lord change me according to what He had told me at your retreat. And it really worked. Now there is someone else I need to pray my 'Lord, change me' prayer about."

"There surely is," agreed her smiling husband.

ALL-CHURCH PRAYER WEEK

Conduct an all-church prayer week with God speaking instead of people? To do this took courage, but the results of our "Lord, change me" prayer week in January were fantastic. We observed a strict rule of no preparation, no leading. The week before, we trained all those who would be leading the groups. If they had not had an experience of God speaking personally to them from His Word, they were to find others to lead for them. We formed no new prayer meetings, but used only the existing classes, organizations, and boards of our church as groups.

Spreading this "Lord, change me" process to the whole church resulted in great things. One Sunday School superintendent said, "Every member of the Christian Education board had been in a different preparation week prayer meeting, so our chairman had each share how God had already spoken and changed his life. Each one gave a specific request from his area; then we all prayed about it. Nobody was pulling for his pet project; all prayed only for what God wanted done through the C.E. board. There's a different feeling in the C.E. board now."

A woman who had been at the center of our church's prayer life for several years said, "As I walked into the church and saw the 'Silence, Please' signs, sensed the reverence and hush, and then saw the sanctuary set up for prayer with circles of chairs even on the platform, I felt as if something new was coming to our church." And it did. We used the

"Lord,—change—me" Bible-reading process and our "six S" prayer method—subject by subject, short prayers, simple prayers, specific prayer requests, silent periods, small groups. And we had almost 100 percent participation in audible prayer, and at least five times as many people attended as had ever come before.

Our children's worker said, "As a church staff, our feet really never touched the ground as we led several training sessions a day during preparation week and watched hearts, attitudes, and lives change as God spoke and these leaders were being prepared by Him to lead prayer week meetings in their respective groups. By the time we got to our weekly church staff prayer meeting during the prayer week, there was such a sense of God's presence that tears replaced audible praying."

The results of my fourteen agonizing months of letting God change me privately can well be summed up in the words of our deacon chairman when he reported about that first all-church "Lord,—change—me" prayer week: "The tremendous problems we faced ceased to be problems because of prayer week. We found a unification of spirit that never had been in our board before. Our meeting ended with all of us standing in a circle, holding hands, and singing 'Blest Be the Tie That Binds'—with tears flowing. God moved in that meeting. It was 'preparation week,' with God preparing hearts, that made the difference. I think every church meeting should be run like this."

4

Changed—When I Study God's Word

S hould I let God change me through devotional reading or Bible study?" That is not a fair question, because *both* are essential for a well-rounded, transformed life. Devotional reading is never a substitute for deep, systematic Bible study—but it is a complement to it. And the Lord does change me *when I study His Word.*

Paul gave Timothy excellent advice when he said, "Study to show thyself approved unto God" (2 Tim. 2:15). He also counseled him to: "Remember that from early childhood you have been familiar with the sacred writings which have power to make you wise and lead you to salvation through faith in Christ Jesus. Every inspired Scripture has its use for *teaching* the truth and *refuting* error, or for *reformation of manners and discipline in right living,* so that the man who belongs to God may be efficient and equipped for good work of every kind" (2 Tim. 3:15–16, NEB, italics mine).

I'm so grateful that God did not ask me to give up teaching when I prayed that He would make me the kind of wife He wanted me to be, for this would have deprived me of great joy. Digging into the Bible always produces a joy and an excitement that *changes* me into a different person. My spiritual barometer, 1 John 1:4, applies here, "These things [are written] … that your joy [might] be full." Even if I'm willing to be changed by what God is teaching me, the end result is always joy. Deep Bible study also produces spiritual maturity—Christ-likeness—in me.

One of the guidelines we gave to each participant of Key '73 neighborhood Bible studies was "The purpose of this study is for us to find our lifestyle out of God's Word. This will include accurately observing what the Bible really says and applying it to our lives."

This chapter is not intended to be an in-depth guide on how to study the Bible. Its purpose is to show how life-changing a thorough study of God's Word can be. Here are some guidelines:

PRE-STUDY PRAYER

As I study God's Word, approximately one third of the study time is spent in prayer. This prayer time is divided into four categories: before the study, while observing what the Scripture really says, while interpreting what it means, and when applying it to myself or those whom I'm teaching.

Just approaching my study time in prayer *changes me.* First, I pray about my personal preparation. Praying for *cleansing* before starting to study establishes a clear communication with God. Then expressing in prayer the hunger and thirst after righteousness that I feel in my heart assures me of "God's filling" (Matt. 5:6).

Next, it is important for me to pray, "Lord, *remove all preconceived ideas* about this portion of Scripture I am about to study." It is always possible that something I have heard or studied previously has not been correct. Praying for God to remove all preconceived ideas (for the study time) will enable Him to reveal fresh insights to me. I let my spirit soar as I thrill at new thoughts from His Word!

I also pray that God will *take control* of the study time so that all observations, interpretations, and applications will be *truth*. I must acknowledge my dependence upon Him if I want accurate, powerful, life-changing lessons for myself or those I will be teaching.

Then, *I ask God to be my Teacher*, inviting the Holy Spirit to be operative in me as I study. In John 14:26 Jesus said that the Holy Spirit would "teach you all things." Also, Paul prayed for the Christians at Ephesus that God would give them "the spirit of wisdom and revelation in the knowledge of Him, [that] the eyes of [their] understanding being enlightened; that [they] may know what is the hope of his calling" (Eph. 1:17–18). The Bible is more than a textbook of poetry, history, psychology, law, and letters; it is a living, personal message from God's heart to our hearts! And studying it thoroughly, deeply, and systematically produces *changed* people.

A good Bible study always includes three elements: *observation, interpretation,* and *application.* And as I diligently practice each part, God *changes me.*

I. OBSERVATION
A. For Teachers
A great change comes over me as a teacher when I admit my fallibility. Having prayed for God to remove all my preconceived ideas, I am thereby made teachable. Then as I read the Scripture portion to be studied, I *observe* carefully what it really says, admitting the possibility of incorrect or incomplete preconceived ideas.

Since my experience in Hebrews 12 when Judy died, I am convinced that God not only allows suffering but that He sends chastening our way. It is He who is doing the chastening. But because this is an unpopular truth with many Christians, I found myself at one time watering down this concept to "God allowing, not sending" in order to accommodate them. But while studying for my Bible class in 1 Peter, I was greatly relieved to observe the phrase: "Let them that suffer according to the will of God" (4:19). This observation changed me into a much more confident teacher—having found confirmation of what God had taught me years before. So many of our ideas are built on what we think the Bible says, rather than on what it actually does say.

As I studied for that Bible class, God gave me some additional help in 1 Peter 3:1 for my fourteen months of living "without a word" before my daughter. For the first time I noticed how that verse started: "In the same way" (NASB) which referred me back to something that came before. (This is like "therefore," showing what a statement is "there for.") As I checked the preceding verses, I found that wives are to act in the same manner as Jesus did in His suffering. He, who did no sin and in whose mouth was found no guile, didn't retaliate when He was reviled or threaten when He suffered. No, Jesus just committed Himself to God who judges righteously (2:22–23). I had additional changing to do—to become more Christ-like.

Then as I passed this observation on to my class members, two of them, whose husbands were being unfaithful, also saw God's answer for their own needs. When they reacted in a way that pleased God, they too could commit themselves and their problems to Him, the faithful and right-eous Judge.

Pronouns are particularly tricky little words: They can tell us a whole story, for example: On Resurrection morning the angel, talking to the women at the tomb, said, "Remember how He [Jesus] spoke unto you when He was yet in Galilee, saying, 'The Son of man must be delivered into the hands of sinful men, and be crucified, and the third day rise again'" (Luke 24:6–7). That "you" tells us a whole story: (1) The women traveled with Jesus and ministered to Him in Galilee. (2) Jesus gave this teaching to the women (the angel doesn't mention the men to whom this most likely was given also). (3) Jesus taught the women directly while they traveled with Him to Jerusalem. (4) Jesus entrusted the women with some very important teaching. This little pronoun refuted several of my preconceived ideas about the place of women in the ministry of Jesus and changed my thinking considerably.

Plural pronouns can be enlightening. By observing the "us" in 2 Corinthians 2:11 I saw that Paul was talking about *himself* and the Christians at Corinth. "Lest Satan should get an advantage of us." I then realized that if Paul wasn't safe from the toehold of Satan in his rela-tionship with the Corinthian Christians, I had better be a little more alert.

Changed by a plural pronoun!

A teacher can get an accurate understanding of a situation by observing verbs. In Matthew 14:22 we read that after His baptism "Jesus constrained His disciples to get into a ship and to go before Him unto the other side." Since Jesus deliberately sent His disciples into the storm, I reassessed my attitude toward the storms in my life. Does Jesus deliberately send me into storms so that I too can see the miracle of His walking on the water and the storm stilled?

Then again the little verb "drove" encompassed a whole theological truth. In Mark 1:12 we observe that "the Spirit immediately drove Him [Jesus] out into the wilderness" (RSV). And He was there forty days, tested by Satan. Again my preconceived idea had to be changed by one little verb. The Spirit didn't *hinder* Him from going, didn't *allow* Jesus to go; no, the Spirit *drove* Jesus to His temptation by Satan.

Another important rule for teachers to follow is: "Read the Scripture portion *before* reading any lesson helps. Carefully observing all God's Word has to say in the study enables teachers to evaluate lesson helps and commentaries in the light of the Scriptures."

Unless we actually observe first what the Scripture says, we are apt to accept gullibly all the teachings in other books—right or wrong, and be changed by them—rightly or wrongly.

Accurately observing everything God says in an assigned portion of Scripture is the opposite of teaching by the piecemeal methods, where a teacher skips through the Bible, taking a verse or part of a verse to prove a point. (This may be an acceptable method if each section has been carefully studied in context and if the premise to be proved is scripturally accurate.) Isolated phrases and sentences put together at a teacher's whim can be made to prove almost anything.

When my neighbor was evaluating some Bible class study samples I had given her, she said to me, "We chose this one because it takes a portion of Scripture and teaches what it says. We don't like to jump around. If I took a bunch of letters from someone, cut out sentences here and there, and put them together the way I wanted, I could prove anything I cared to!"

While teaching this process to some senior highers, I evidently got a little carried away with my proving, for after Sunday School I received a phone call from an upset father. "What do you mean teaching our son that all the demons will be saved?" I hurried to explain that I was teaching the young people how *not* to prove something about demons. I had put three "pieces" of Scripture together—all true in their proper setting—and thereby "proved" that all demons will be saved.

1. "I know Thee who Thou art, the Holy One of God" (unclean spirit's words in Mark 1:24).
2. "The demons also believe, and tremble" (James 2:19).
3. "Believe on the Lord Jesus, and thou shalt be saved" (Acts 16:31).

Even the Scriptures themselves can be used to change us in a way that is contrary to God's truth and His will if we don't observe accurately what they say, all they say, and in context. We can be changed incorrectly by the Bible!

B. For Those I Teach

Lorna and Signe, my two prayer partners at that time, and I prayed for two years that I might teach a neighborhood evangelism Bible study class. But I had some changing to do before God would allow me to teach. I had to learn that the pupils too had the right to observe what God was saying to them and not to rely solely on what their teacher said. If I had used my lecture method, I would have given them what God had taught me through His Word instead of allowing them to discover for themselves what the Bible teaches. When I learned at last that the purpose of a Bible study is to let God be the Teacher, He gave me a wonderful class to teach every week.

When we came together in Ruth's living room, we first of all prayed that God would remove our preconceived ideas so that He could speak to our specific needs.

Then we read individually—silently—the Scripture we were to study that day, so that the teacher or whoever else might be reading aloud would not emphasize the words *they* wanted stressed. I offered no hints as to what God might say to them.

And this wasn't just a casual reading. It was the process described in James 1:25 of "looking into the perfect law of liberty" which meant seeking, desiring, longing for, as when Mary "looked" into the empty tomb that first Easter morning.

We had women from all denominations and walks of life in that Bible study, but none was a skilled Bible student. When they finished reading after our second lesson I asked, "Did God say anything to you that you didn't know before?" And 100 percent of them said yes with gusto.

Later, after the reading, I introduced the teaching with, "What did God tell you?" They exploded with excitement. One lady tried to count on her fingers all the things God had said, but she didn't have enough fingers. I almost lost control of the group as they all talked at once. *They* had been taught by God!

Early in the study I learned how to make those who had never studied the Bible before feel that they were a part of the discussion. I would ask them the "observation" question and, just from reading carefully, they would be able to answer intelligently on what the Scripture had really said.

We had one very quiet member who sat through our first lessons too shy to say a word. But all at once God spoke to her through the simple three-letter word "saw." The fact that Jesus "saw" people burst upon her— how He *saw* Peter and Andrew and James and John. Then she commented that she was at the Bible study because so-and-so "saw" her and asked her to attend, but moved away before the study started. But another person "saw" her and picked her up and brought her here to study the Bible. After almost twenty minutes she stopped abruptly and apologized for monopolizing so much time. She had gained insight into Scripture—just by observing a little verb!

A teacher is humbled when God speaks dramatically to the class before she even gives her introductory remarks. That happened to me as I asked my usual, "Did God say anything to you?" question, and one member said, "Yes, He did."

"What did He say?"

"He said that I didn't know the Scriptures. Well, that's why I'm here—because my church doesn't teach the Bible and I want to learn the Scriptures. But God also said, 'You don't know the power of God either!'" (cf. Mark 12:24)

"Would you like to know the power of God?"

"Yes, I would."

"Right now?" (After all, we hadn't even started the lesson yet, and it certainly wasn't time for application.)

"Yes, right now." And before I even started to teach she bowed her head and accepted Jesus as her Savior. *Changed*—just by observing the Word. Yes, God had some *changing* to do in me with this method of Bible study as well as in the pupils I was teaching.

Another important fact to *observe* while studying God's Word is "to whom a portion of Scripture is written." It makes a lot of difference who needs to be changed and also who is eligible to apply the Scripture to his life. At a Bible study in St. Paul, a woman observed "the eyes of your understanding being enlightened" from Ephesians 1:18.

"My family is not getting along well. How can the eyes of my understanding be enlightened so I will know how to run it better?"

"To whom did we learn this book was written?"

"To the saints which are at Ephesus and to the faithful in Christ Jesus" (Eph. 1:1).

"Are you a saint—one who knows Jesus as personal Savior? Are you *in* Christ Jesus?"

"No."

"Then you are not eligible for what Paul was praying for."

And at that she decided to accept Christ—right there!

A well-known Christian author and speaker said to me, as we were discussing the way God speaks so specifically out of His Word, "Do you mean to tell me that somebody can find Christ just by reading the Bible?"

"Yes, sir, it really works."

II. INTERPRETATION

If I'm going to understand and interpret the Bible accurately, I must spend time studying its meaning in addition to observing what the text says. I must rely on Bible scholars for word meanings from original manuscripts and for information on how the cultural setting influenced what was written.

Also, God has spoken to Christians down through the ages, and my failure to study what He has revealed to them makes me poor indeed. I am immeasurably richer when I learn from them, and am inspired by the insights they have gleaned. The early church learned these things immediately, for we find in Acts 2:42 that the new Christians "continued steadfastly in the *apostles' doctrine* and fellowship, and in breaking of bread, and in prayers."

And years later Paul admonished young Timothy to "give attendance to reading, to exhortation, to doctrine" (1 Tim. 4:13). In the interpretation we study in depth the meaning of a passage. Minimum study aids include a good commentary, a Bible dictionary, a Bible atlas, and a scholarly dictionary for word study.

God changes me into a *disciplined* person when I obey the command of 2 Timothy 2:15: "Study to shew thyself approved unto God, a workman that needeth not to be ashamed, rightly dividing the word of truth." To study takes discipline. Research is hard work, and time-consuming. It demands a reassessment of priorities—the giving up of some shopping trips, coffee parties, entertainment and recreation—some "good" but not "best" things.

Prayer at this point is essential. In order to be changed by my study the way God wants me to change, I pray, asking God to guard my mind as I read. Just because something is in print doesn't make it true. Then I pray for God to help me be selective. "Lord, lead me to just the books You want me to study." Indiscriminate reading of every book on a subject may not be good stewardship of my time, so I ask Him to show me what will be relevant to me and to those I will be teaching. Then I pray for His wisdom in interpreting and understanding the correct meaning. My greatest insight frequently comes not from reading but from praying.

But there must be a *proper balance* between inspiration and perspiration. I used to bring home all the reference books from my pastor husband's library for the study of next Sunday's lesson, stack them on the dining room table (the pile usually was at least two feet high), and systematically wade through them all that week. Then, after up to 25 hours of study, by Saturday I was ready to put the gleaned wisdom into outline form, dash it off to the church secretary to be mimeographed for the class members, and then go home to pray, "Dear God, please bless my notes."

I asked God to change that procedure, and He did. He taught me there was a proper balance between what other people had to say and what He had to say. A seminary senior, in tears, confided to me, "I've dissected the Scriptures so long that they don't say anything to me any more." My own college botany professor gave us some profound advice: "Remember, after you do enough dissecting, you no longer have a flower."

But there is also the danger of all observation with little or no perspiration. By striking a happy medium and not neglecting either, God produced a good balance for me. To maintain this balance, I developed a *work sheet* on which I systematically recorded the various aspects of my lesson preparation. In three vertical columns I recorded: (1) my observations, (2) what it means to those to whom the passage was written and the meaning to us today, and (3) the application for me and for those I teach. This assured me of change through all aspects of study.

Interpretation of the Scripture portion is divided into two categories: (A) What it meant to those to whom it was written, and (B) what it means today.

A. What It Meant to Those to Whom It Was Written

God changes my attitude toward Bible teachings when I understand their actual meanings. The meanings of words change through the years, and only by relying on scholars who have studied original meanings can I be assured of accurate understanding. Comparing several of the good translations is helpful also. To insure accurate instruction I must remember that paraphrases are good, understandable Bible helps, but not literal translations. I also keep in mind to whom the portion was written. Does 1 John 1:8 apply to non-Christians, or was it written only to Christians? And when the psalmist prayed, "Take not Thy Holy Spirit from me" (51:11), he was writing before Pentecost, so that it is not a way I ask God to change me today. Then too I must not assume that I can be changed by the study of only one portion of Scripture on a certain theme. I must study all His Word teaches on that subject, and not insist on being changed only by my "pet" Scripture.

B. *What It Means to Us Today*

Only in the light of what the Scripture meant to those to whom it was written can I know accurately what it should mean to me today. We tend to interpret God's commands and instructions in the light of culture trends in the church and in our world. When I started teaching my first neighborhood Bible study I had to deal almost immediately with the cultures of different churches.

When someone asked the question, "What is sin?" the answers started flowing. "My church believes you can have one cocktail at a wedding reception." ... "My church allows alcoholic beverages for all adults." ... "My church only allows beer and wine." ... "We don't believe in any alcohol!" After agreeing to the rule that we would take as authoritative only what the Bible said and not what churches believed, the problem disappeared.

Then we are prone to put emphasis on "today," thinking that the moral climate of the age somehow influences what God demands of us. I remember hearing sermons condemning television sets when they first came out. My husband recalls that when he was a little child, his grandfather stormed into his home after his father had bought the first radio in the neighborhood, saying, "Well, I never thought I'd see my son on the way to hell." But attitudes change. Most of those who once violently condemned movies now sit glued to their TV sets as old reruns flash right into their living rooms.

God gave our Nancy a good answer to this problem when she was a teenager.

"Mother, is what was sin when you were a girl still sin?"

"Where are you reading in God's Word these days?" I asked.

"Ephesians."

"Let's take that book and see what God says."

So, as we had done many times before, we both read silently until He stopped one of us. Suddenly Nancy said, "Stop. God gave me the answer in verse 4."

"What did He say?"

"'That we should be holy and without blame before Him.' It doesn't make any difference whether we lived at the time Christ was on earth or a 100 years ago, or whether we live today, we are to be blameless and acceptable in His sight."

God's standard does not change—His yardstick of perfection is not shortened by years or culture; His purpose to conform me to the image of Christ is the same yesterday, today, and forever. When I know what God's instructions really meant to those to whom they were written, I can apply the same truths to my life today.

III. APPLICATION

The real change in me comes when I take the truths I have observed and studied and *apply* them to my life. Only when I apply the Scripture does God do the actual changing in my thinking and my actions.

There are reasons for reading the Bible historically as an overview of a book or the whole Bible. But the real life-changing come when we apply, one by one, the precepts that He tells us. "Precept upon precept; line upon line" (Isa. 28:10).

I had been teaching the same Sunday School class of sharp young adults for about twelve years when an unsettling thought started gnawing away at me: "Are those people any different because of all my hours of perspiring in lesson preparation?" Oh, they were a great group, and I would come away from class with a heady sense of exhilaration from the lively give-and-take discussion on deep biblical subjects. In fact, that class was one of the joys of my life.

But the gnawing persisted—was actually growing—were they really different because of all my efforts?

Then the officers and I met to plan the year's program and curriculum. And I dropped the bomb. "I'm not going to teach this class any more unless I see more evidence that the Scriptures are actually changing lives."

The only audible response was the swallowing of the others in the room. The stunned silence didn't deter me. I launched our paragraph by paragraph study of the Book of Mark with a new determination. Either they would let God *change* them by what we were studying from His Word or I was finished as their teacher!

After a couple of months, one Sunday morning I announced to the class that, instead of studying that day's lesson, I wanted them to share with all of us exactly how God had changed them by specific lessons we had studied. It didn't take long to see that God had been at work. One after another stood to share what God had changed in them because of specific Scriptures we had studied. My apprehension and fears were over. They *had* to let God change them. Then Bill, our class president, looked at me and said rather meekly, "Did we tell you enough so you'll keep teaching, Ev?"

I remember the advice on counseling that Dr. Henry Brandt gave to the international leaders at the Expo '72 Convention: "Only listen till the people coming for counseling mention a scriptural precept they're violating. Stop their conversation and give them the scriptural answer. Then send them off, telling them not to come back for more advice until they have *lived and applied* that answer."

During one of my neighborhood Bible studies, the women all were suffering from deep personal family trials. But as we studied the Book of First Peter, we found an amazing thing happening. God gave answers *to live by* week after week to those who seemed to need help the most. I watched as they observed that those early Christians were suffering for a season but were to rejoice as the testing of their faith was preparing them for Jesus' return (1 Peter 1:6–7). The women's attitude toward their problems changed as they applied this truth. They actually learned to smile again.

Most of the women were enduring undeserved suffering (2:20), which was being caused by another family member. And I watched them change from being resentful, defensive, and wanting to retaliate to TAKING IT PATIENTLY because Christ was their Example of suffering although innocent of wrongdoing. They applied what they studied.

But they were also watching for changes in me, their teacher, for I too was going through a deep family trial. One day while studying 1 Peter 4:19 for the lesson, "Wherefore let them that suffer according to the will of God *commit* the keeping of their souls to Him," I discovered that the word translated "commit" was the same word as was translated "commend" in Luke 23:46. Jesus, agonizing as He gave up His spirit on the cross, cried with a loud voice and said, "Father, into Thy hands I commend My spirit." How God lifted my burden as I applied that truth to my own life! Although my suffering was so small compared to that of my Christ on the cross, I, with Him, committed the keeping of my soul to God. And He changed me.

I cannot expect those I teach to be changed by applying God's Word if I have not been changed by it first. But that is exactly what happens when I study His Word. The observations are thrilling, the study is exhilarating, but the *change* comes when I personally apply what the Scripture means to my everyday life. The "Lord, change me" comes when I let His word abide, take up residence, in me (John 15:7). The change comes when I am a doer of the Word and not a hearer only (James 1:22–25). For when I look into the Bible and do not apply it, I am like a person beholding my face in a mirror and immediately forgetting the mess I see. But when I look into God's Word and do what it says, then I am changed into a blessed person. Changed—when I study His Word.

5

Changed—When the Holy Spirit Reminds

*M*any times God wants to change me when I'm reading or study-ing His Word, or when I'm with a group "reading until He speaks." But when I find myself in a situation where I need help imme-diately, then the Holy Spirit brings to my mind the Scripture that meets my need at that moment. One of the primary reasons for read-ing and studying the Bible is to provide Him with the Word to bring to our remembrance—*when we need it.*

Jesus said: "These things have I spoken unto you, being yet present with you. But the Comforter, who is the Holy Spirit, whom the Father will send in My name, He shall teach you all things, *and bring all things to your remembrance*, whatsoever I have said unto you" (John 14:25–26).

Now, some of the disciples would be recording the words of Jesus in some of the books of the New Testament. What a word of assurance this must have been for them. But was this promise of the Spirit's prompting given only to Peter, John, Matthew, and the other disciples who were with Jesus at that time? I think not. Prisoners of war and others who have had Bibles taken from them tell fantastic stories of the Holy Spirit recalling for them the Scriptures they had learned previously. This is one of the most powerful ways God has used the Scriptures down through the ages.

One of the surprises that came out of my analysis and the underlined and dated verses in my three Bibles was that frequently the verse didn't have any immediate specific meaning to me. But when there was a need some time in the future, the Holy Spirit pulled from my memory exactly the portion of Scripture that fitted the need.

We stay in the Bible, studying and reading devotionally, being taught by God so that the Holy Spirit can bring to our remembrance what He has told us. We tell our children that they can't expect God to help them recall answers on a test if they have never studied the material in the first place. Neither can we expect God to bring to our remembrance answers to our needs if we have not stored His truth in our hearts.

A couple of years ago I was fretting because I was remembering less and less as I grew older. But in a moment the Holy Spirit kindly reminded me of this verse on His bringing all things to our remembrance—His way of dealing with old age! Then I thought back on the chat I had with quite forgetful 82-year-old Corrie ten Boom the month before. "Evelyn," she said, "I never forget a spiritual thing."

That I Might Not Sin

I viewed with awe my neighbor across our cul-de-sac who was working on the then world's largest computer. My mind was boggled as he told of the 1 million words it could work on at a time and the billions of facts its memory banks could store. But we as human beings possess the world's most sophisticated and complex memory banks—our minds—and they store up all the information acquired by us from infancy.

The psalmist says: "Thy Word have I hid in mine heart, that I might not sin against Thee" (Ps. 119:11). This is the process of tucking the Word of God deep down in our hearts by study and memorization. As we read the Bible, study it, and listen to sermons from it, we are not to dismiss what God says to us, but are to *hide* those spiritual truths in the deepest recesses of our hearts.

But those of us who know the pain of trying to recall some of the information we stored there as a child (even *old* math), the college material that produced an "A" grade, or even a recipe that seemed so simple twenty years ago, realize the inadequacy of our human memory systems. As human operators we are frequently unable to bring forth even a tiny bit of stored information. But when we need to recall a particular spiritual truth, we have a supernatural computer operator—the Holy Spirit!

When I recognize there is something wrong in my life and I know God wants to change me, I feed the problem into the computer of my mind. Then, when I ask God to give me a solution, the Holy Spirit often *reminds* me of a portion of Scripture—a verse or a single word—that shows me the specific sin that is causing my problem. Many times He flashes back: "pride" (Rom. 12:3) or "worry" (Phil. 4:6).

Occasionally, before I'm even aware that something is wrong, or before I know there is a problem to feed into my computer, my Supernatural Operator is already spelling out an answer to me. He knows the need or the problem before I ask, before I consciously formulate it into words. Jesus said in Matthew 6:8 that our Heavenly Father knows what things we have need of *before* we ask Him, and the solution is recalled from my scriptural memory bank before I spell out my need. That's even less time than the fastest computer in the world takes to summon answers! Yes, before I even realize my sin, the Holy Spirit is reminding, prodding, reproving with His gentle nudge or stating in no uncertain voice, "That's SIN!"

Our Supernatural Operator, the Holy Spirit, never makes a mistake. In one of our Kurt's junior high classes where the computer forms had the classifications "male," "female," and "other," some shocked students were classified as "other" by the not-too-friendly computer. And how I recall the agony of all the "Christensons" getting mixed up on the computer of our city's largest department store, just before our Jan's wedding. With all the shopping we had to do, we were suddenly lost from the face of the earth. And how embarrassed our senior high daughter felt when her school's computer assigned her to a boys' gym class! But the Holy Spirit never makes an error. Even when we feed in the wrong problem, He comes up with exactly the right answer for our specific need.

Reminding me of a scriptural answer when I ask for it, or even before I ask, is one of the methods the Holy Spirit uses to "reprove of sin," as Jesus mentioned in John 16:8. The psalmist in Psalm 119:11 gives the "why" for hiding God's Word in our hearts: "Thy Word have I hid in mine *heart, that I might not sin against Thee.*" How else could God's Word, hidden, unseen, perhaps even forgotten, keep me from sin except that the Holy Spirit *recalls* it? This is the supernatural process of the Holy Spirit, more accurate than any computer that will ever be invented by man, reaching down and *recalling* for me exactly the answer I need from God's Word at the very time I need it.

My Spiritual Operator, the Holy Spirit, has a favorite verse He spells out for me:

"B-E

Y-E

H-O-L-Y;

F-O-R

I

A-M

H-O-L-Y" (1 Peter 1:16).

I hid this verse in my heart many years ago, and I'm surprised it isn't worn out from God's flashing it at me so often. But it gets to me every time. I immediately see my God high and lifted up, holy—perfect attitudes, actions, and reactions. And what I've stored in my memory bank from His Word comes clicking back to me. And I know how holy God is—and how holy I'm expected to be! Recalled—to keep me from sinning.

I remember one day while on vacation at our cottage I had a sudden eye-contact with a man. I flushed slightly, enjoying his obvious approval of me. The next morning I asked God to enlighten my understanding of the sin of this type of encounter. Slowly, as if on a screen in my mind, the words "Be ye holy; for I am holy" came forward until they were in focus. I asked God for complete cleansing, and immediately I was *changed*. Communing with God as He gave me several pieces of wisdom for my next book, I was suddenly engulfed with adoration of Him. Welling up from the depths of my being, flowing into every inch of my body was the prayer, "Oh, God, how good is vacation! Time to drink deeply of Your Word, to read good Christian books. Time to adore You rather than working under the tyranny of the urgent." Changed when the Holy Spirit recalled His "old faithful" verse.

To Comfort Me

The Holy Spirit causes me to remember not only to keep me from sinning but also to supply needs in my life. When I find myself in adverse situations, He provides the Scripture I need to comfort me.

The night before I was to speak four times at a retreat high up in the Rocky Mountains, I was reading my Bible and these words spoke to me, "For He shall give His angels charge over thee, to keep thee in all Thy ways" (Ps. 91:11). Angels? Why did I need angels when I was securely tucked into a warm bed in a nice private trailer?

But the next morning I woke cold and miserable. The electricity, and thus my electric heater, had gone off in the night; and, although it was only September, the first snow of the season had just fallen. Adding to my misery was a hard case of intestinal flu with its accompanying chills. Shivering violently, I piled all the blankets and coats in sight on me, trying to get warm. Then the Holy Spirit suddenly recalled for me the verse I had read the night before. "Angels? Wow, do I ever need them right now!" And just the thought of God sending His angels to hover and watch over me in that room changed me—warmed my spirit and made those difficult circumstances easier to take. His miracle of making me well enough to speak all that day was to come later, but right then I needed the assurance and comfort of the Scripture the Holy Spirit recalled.

While we were traveling overseas a few years ago, I came down with a severe infection in Jerusalem. As I was lying all alone in my hotel bed, looking out on the Mount of Olives, the Holy Spirit reminded me of

Romans 8:28, and I knew that even missing the tour that day was being worked out by God for my good. Then He brought to my remembrance some of the lessons from God's Word that I had tucked down in my heart years before. Again, Romans 8:28—He brought good from the loss of those three pregnancies right after we were married. Then from Hebrews 12—the chapter that was so real to me at the time of Judy's death—He had taught me that even her death was for *my profit*. Lying there, I let God speak afresh about those lessons from His Word of yesteryears.

Surprisingly, instead of lying there rebelling at missing the tour to Bethlehem that day, I found my spirit soaring to the heavenlies with God—*changed!* He enveloped me with a tremendous sense of His presence—caring for and speaking to me personally. I spent hours listening to "Jerusalem sounds"—a cock crowing in the morning, a donkey braying in the distance—and had the unspeakable thrill of seeing the rising sun burst over the Mount of Olives, just as it must have done that first Easter morning! And God proved that the Scriptures He was recalling would work again. Later in the week I was given a tour of Bethlehem by private car, and when I returned to Jerusalem I had the wonderful privilege of spending an hour alone in the Garden of Gethsemane, communing with my Lord.

For Teaching Others

The Holy Spirit frequently brings to my remembrance Scripture I have hidden in my heart so that I can teach others the truths God has taught me.

Back in 1957 I was scheduled to speak at a women's meeting but could not get a message I felt God wanted me to bring them; every idea I had seemed inadequate. In desperation I arose early on the morning of the day I was to bring the message and sought out my old green "prayer" chair. Prayer and searching God's Word produced nothing. Finally, in exasperation, I laid aside my Bible and picked up the newspaper. The headlines stunned me. Russia had sent Sputnik I into outer space! The frenzied race to *conquer* outer space was on. (How foolish that word "conquer" sounds now.) President Eisenhower, astonished that the Russians had projectors and propellants which could cast that 184-pound object into outer space, gave a message of comfort and encouragement to the American people on the front page.

But almost immediately the Holy Spirit recalled a portion of Scripture that I had hidden deep in my heart when I had taught the book of Colossians to my Sunday School class: "For by Him [Jesus] were all things created, that are in heaven, and that are in earth, visible and invisible, whether they be thrones, or dominions, or principalities, or powers; all things were created by Him, and for Him; and He is before all things, and by Him all things consist" (Col. 1:16–17).

I had my message! Jesus *made* outer space! He put the stars and planets, the sun and the moon in place! Jesus *holds* them all together! He makes them run on course according to His will! We are not to fear some nation that can make a little piece of hardware circling our planet. But we are to put our trust in the One who created all of that outer space, the One by whom it all consists—Jesus!

Just by recalling a portion of Scripture, that whole shocking news item came into focus. It lost its horror. I could go to that meeting and tell those frightened women that our enemy had invaded outer space before us, but Jesus had been out there creating it and controlling it from eternity past! *Changed*—when the Holy Spirit brought just two verses to my remembrance.

The Holy Spirit also recalled a precious portion when I was asked to speak to a women's Sunday School class in Ambo, Ethiopia. None of them understood English, and I wondered what we had in common that I could talk about. As I looked out the window of their church, I saw a mountain in the distance. And immediately the Holy Spirit brought to mind *my* mountain verses from Psalm 121. They understood mountains!

Slowly, with the help of an interpreter, I related the story of how God spoke to me on my mountain. I told them that after having a slight heart problem I had gone to a doctor to find out whether it was advisable for me to travel through the high Rocky Mountains in Canada on my way to Vancouver, British Columbia. A group of us were traveling in a caravan of cars, and everything went fine until we reached our first mountain. Suddenly I had trouble breathing and my heart started to beat wildly. We stopped at a motel and, while the others went to a restaurant, I spent the time in bed, gazing out at huge Cascade Mountain, which seemed to go straight up from my bedroom window. "O, God," I prayed, "please give me just the Scripture You want me to read. I don't want to be sick and unable to go on to Vancouver. I don't want to break up the caravan. Please give me something from Your Word." Then God flashed Psalm 121:1–2 in my mind. I reached for my Bible and read: "I will lift up mine eyes unto the hills, from whence cometh my help. My help cometh from the Lord, which made heaven and earth."

Then I told those Ethiopian ladies, "I was looking up to the hills, but they hadn't helped me. In fact, they had caused my heart to act strangely. But there's a question mark after verse one; my answer was in the next verse. My help comes from the Lord who *made* those high mountains. Then I decided to trust God for all the strength I would need to get across those mountains, and right away my heart was OK." Changed!

I told those Ethiopian women that when it was time for devotions the next morning I had the caravan stop on another one of those big mountains, and we all sat down while I read my "mountain verses" to them, telling them of my trust in the God who made all the mountains and who made—and keeps—me. Yes, the Holy Spirit had recalled just the Scripture I needed to teach that Sunday School in Africa that morning.

When I was doing follow-up counseling after a citywide youth evangelism week, I was happy that I had tucked some verses down in my heart. On the last night the leader announced, "Mrs. Christenson will take all those who have finished their written follow-up books and teach them." My mind raced. How could I fill up a whole evening with teaching when all the subjects had been completed by these high schoolers? When a newspaper editor asked to interview a few of my young people, I silently thanked God for the few minutes I had to ask Him what I should tell them.

Then the Holy Spirit recalled several scriptural truths I could share. Changed, I confidently told them that their completed follow-up program didn't mean that the battle was over for them as new Christians (Eph. 6). I reminded them that although temptation would come their way, there is always victory in Jesus (Phil. 4:13), and from 1 John I showed them that when we *do* sin God will forgive us if we confess it to Him (1 John 1:8–9). Then I shared how God would take all of these things, both good and bad, and work them all out for our good (Rom. 8:28).

When the evening was over, one of the other counselors came to me and said, "Whew! I'm glad He didn't give *me* that job. I don't even *know* those verses!"

How important it is to hide God's Word in our hearts so the Holy Spirit can recall it when we need to teach others. It is so great to keep sensitive to the Holy Spirit while teaching and speaking so that He can recall just the Scripture somebody in the audience needs.

JUST FOR ME

Sometimes the Holy Spirit recalls Scripture that is just for me. I'm not going to teach or share it with anyone—it's just for me.

As we drove down to Bethlehem that day I was given a private tour, I prayed "Lord, bring to my mind the Scripture You want me to hear as I view the birthplace of my Savior."

Looking at the shepherds' fields I expected to hear, "And suddenly there was with the angel a multitude of the heavenly host praising God" (Luke 2:13). But no Scripture came to my mind. And as we approached the town of Bethlehem, I waited for Him to recall Micah 5:2, "But thou, Bethlehem Ephratah." But there was nothing. I strained to hear God say something as we approached the Church of the Nativity—nothing. Then on the marble steps descending to the actual stable level—nothing. Breathlessly expectant, I stepped into the room where tradition states Jesus was born. Even as I pulled back the velvet wall hangings and touched the wall—there was still nothing. Regretfully, I walked up the stairs. Not one portion of Scripture recalled especially by God in that precious spot. But as I stepped out into the sunlight of the courtyard once more—it hit! God recalled a total surprise: "And the Word was made flesh, and dwelt among *us*, and we beheld His glory, the glory as of the only begotten of the Father, full of grace and truth" (John 1:14).

The emphasis the Holy Spirit conveyed was on the word "us." I recoiled as my mind went to "me" with my filled teeth, eyeglasses, infection, and recent surgery. Then I looked around at the hunger and pain so prevalent in the Holy Land. Among us? As I almost felt the dirt around me, I wondered at that "Holy Thing" announced by the angel to Mary, being born into this. Yes, a part of it through the birth process. He *dwelt* among *us*?

Then God took my mind back to the preceding verses in that chapter of John. Jesus Christ, who was God, and who had been with God from the beginning—in heaven's perfect environment where there was no pain, sickness, or death—had come down to earth right at that spot and dwelt *among us*. What a new picture God had given me of my Jesus—not the traditional Babe in the manger—but the holy Son of God who loved me enough to come down here and dwell among us. I was completely *changed*—with a new and deep appreciation of my Savior's sacrifice—for me!

I've heard of some awful things that are supposed to happen to parents when the last child leaves the nest. The divorce rate for parents in this category goes up, and many mothers fall into an "I'm-not-needed-any-more" depression. Just before leaving for college, our Kurt said to me, "I think this is harder on you than it is on me, Mother."

Two days after he left, Chris and I were driving along holding hands as we returned from a shopping trip that had carried us through what had been our family dinner hour with our children for twenty-six years. I squeezed his hand and smiled as I said, "ye have not, because ye ask not" (James 4:2). The Holy Spirit had given us that verse for the weekend. And there had been some desperate "asking" as we saw Kurt's empty bed, the vacant spaces where his clock radio, stereo, and desk lamp had stood, as we "listened" to the silent bathroom that had resounded so vigorously every morning with splashing shower and buzzing electric comb.

On the last night of prayer together with Kurt, as we thanked God for the almost eighteen years of joy, and then gave our son to God in a new and special way to make his own life outside our nest, I turned to a new kind of "asking": "Dear God, fill the void with Yourself," I prayed over and over. Then my prayer progressed, adding another dimension: "Dear Father, fill the void with *You and Chris*."

The results were incredible. God filled my life to overflowing with Himself and His love through other people. And after reading about

Joseph taking such good care of the infant Jesus and His mother Mary, I prayed, "Thank You, Lord, for the way Chris protects me and the security I have in him."

Later that week Chris and I traveled together as far as Denver where I was to speak. Before he took off for the rest of his journey to California, he sat on the edge of the bed and said to me, "I don't know or understand all that is happening to us, but I sure like it."

"Ye have not because ye ask not," said the Holy Spirit. And how right He was! I was a completely changed mother and wife—just because I obeyed the Scripture the Holy Spirit recalled.

NUMBER ONE

But Romans 8:28 is by far the number one verse the Holy Spirit recalls for me. In fact, He has reminded me of it so often that I have finally adopted it as my philosophy of life: "And we know that all things work together for good to them that love God, to them who are the called according to His purpose." God gave that verse to me at the time I lost my third pregnancy during our college days. He must have known then how my whole life would revolve around that verse—though I certainly didn't know it at the time.

I used to have to struggle to find the "good" in the seeming calamities of my life, but sooner or later I was able to see what God was doing and why He was doing it. And more and more through the years I am able to see the "why" of circumstances as soon as the Holy Spirit says, "Romans 8:28." What used to take time to figure out, now seems to come almost immediately and automatically.

And it works 100 percent of the time. When something especially bad happens, when the roof caves in or the floor falls out from under me, the Holy Spirit still persists, "*All* things." I cannot accept it just 90 percent of the time or even 98 percent of the time. I must accept it *all* of the time. It was hard at first, but as the years have come and gone, it has become easier. It is a matter of faith. As faith is exercised, it grows stronger and stronger. And the faith, of course, isn't in a verse or even a verse turned into a philosophy of life. The faith is in the God of that verse—the One who is working out all things for my good. And the

Holy Spirit is really recalling not a verse, but all that God has worked out for me for many years.

One of the greatest ways God changes me is by bringing Scripture to mind I have hidden deep in my heart. And He always picks the right Scripture at the right time. What a reason for staying in His Word daily—reading, studying, devouring it. And then what a challenge to stay so sensitive to the Holy Spirit's speaking that He can reach down and recall just exactly what I need at the very minute I need it!

6

Exchange—When I Ask God in Prayer

*A*nswering my prayers for myself is one of the most direct ways God changes me. When I ask Him to change some specific trait in me, He frequently lifts that thing out and replaces it with a quality that He desires me to have. As God removes an attitude, a personality trait, or some characteristic of my old nature, and puts in its place His own attribute, the process is a dramatic one. He does not add a little of His strength to my weakness, or a little of His forgiveness to cover my sin. No, there is an actual *exchange* that takes place within me.

And this exchange takes place when I ask Him in prayer. Of course, the key to this process is my *wanting* Him to change me. Now, God's methods aren't always painless, but the end result is an exchange within me, which leaves me with an unexplainable sense of well being. It is a life-changing process that fills me with His peace, joy, and power—when I ask.

STRENGTH FOR WEAKNESS

Often we ask God to change us, but then don't *wait* for Him to answer our prayer. A secret I learned many years ago is that God gives me some things only *when I wait.*

Recently in a series of hectic days I had an unusually strenuous one. I drove to Wisconsin for an all-day seminar, lectured for six hours, and then drove back home to Minnesota. I had just one-half hour to cook my dinner, eat, and get back on the road for another two-and-a-half hour lecture. At bedtime, Chris, knowing my rigorous schedule, called me from his travels in Florida. "Just wanted to know how you made it through the day, Honey. How was it?"

"Oh, Chris, all I can say is that it was another miracle. By the time I had driven home from Wisconsin I was so exhausted that I could hardly raise my arms, my stomach was hurting, and it was hard to think straight. But, when I started to speak at Bethel College tonight, I suddenly felt as fresh as if I had had eight hours of sound sleep!"

What had happened? Before the evening seminar I took a few minutes to lie down and pray these words: "O God, *exchange* my exhaustion for Your strength." And it worked. God miraculously reached down, lifted my exhaustion, and then replaced it with His strength.

The same thing happened to me a few months ago at the greater Los Angeles Sunday School Convention. The night before I left I had taught all evening, driven fifty miles, arrived home at midnight, and then had packed for the trip to Los Angeles. Early the next morning I flew out to California and dashed into the convention center just minutes before I was to speak. That evening I was scheduled to give my final lecture of that day at 8:30 P.M. California time. But that was 10:30 P.M. according to the time on which I was operating! Start again at 10:30? And continue lecturing until *my* 11:45?

During a short break between sessions, I dashed to my motel room, and suddenly realized that my staggering schedule had caught up with my body—my head felt fuzzy, and I was shaking all over. So I went to prayer—not just asking but desperately hanging on to God for help. Here again I practiced that threefold formula which never fails: 1. *Stop.* 2. *Ask.* 3. *Wait.* The results were fantastic. I bounced over to that final meeting and never felt a speck of fatigue all through the session!

Dr. Stephen Olford in his booklet, *The Secret of Strength*, explains that the word "renew" in Isaiah 40:31 ("They that wait upon the Lord shall renew their strength") actually means "the process by which the molting eagle *exchanges* its old feathers for new ones." We think of the renewing process as an addition of a little strength, but to God it is an actual replacement.

When we are fatigued, our tendency is to keep pushing and pushing, slower and slower, until we get the job done. But God's formula is so simple. And it takes such a short time to stop, ask, and wait. However, there is a key to this formula: Ask, and then wait expectantly. This requires *faith*—not in the few minutes I might have in which to rest, but in the *One* who is to provide the strength. Hebrews 11:6 explains it so clearly: "But without faith it is impossible to please Him; for he that cometh to God must believe that He is, and that He is a Rewarder of them that diligently seek Him." It is God who *exchanges* my fatigue for His strength. And He does it when I stop, ask in faith, and wait expectantly.

THE MIND OF CHRIST FOR MY FALLIBILITY

Another exchange takes place in me when I acknowledge my inadequate ideas, my shortcomings or sinful attitudes, and ask God for the *mind of Christ.*

The first step in this process is to recognize that there is something more or something better than I am now experiencing. My needs can be difficult to detect, for my inadequate thoughts frequently disguise a deeper problem, my shortcomings often excuse inactivity, and sometimes my sins actually feel good. When I finally acknowledge that something is wrong, then I can *ask* for the mind of Christ.

The day before I started a prayer seminar in the largest Lutheran church in the world, my son-in-law phoned and said, "Do you want to hear a funny story?"

"Sure," I relied.

"Well, Jan and I were being entertained in a couple's home, and our hostess mentioned Pastor Lyndon Karo. 'How do you know him?' Jan asked in surprise. 'Oh, I read about him in a book on prayer.' 'My mother wrote that book,' said Jan. 'Oh,' said our hostess as she glanced nervously around her house, 'if I had known, I would have cleaned my house better,'"

After Skip and I stopped laughing, he continued. "Then our hostess became quiet and preoccupied with her own thoughts. She blurted out, '*I feel as if I'm entertaining God.*'" And at that Skip and I roared with laughter. That surely was a funny story.

But when I hung up the phone, God said to Evelyn—pride! I dropped to my knees and pled with God to *give me the mind of Christ.* "O God, please forgive me for that terrible attitude. I'm sorry. Please give me the mind of Christ." Immediately God brought Philippians 2 to my mind. I knew what that portion said, but scurried for my Bible so I wouldn't miss a single word: "Let this mind be in you, which was also in Christ Jesus; who being in the form of God, thought it not robbery to be equal with God; but made Himself of no reputation, and took upon Him the form of a servant" (vv. 5–7).

I was overwhelmed. Jesus *was* God (John 1:1). Jan wasn't God. I wasn't God—but Jesus, who actually was God, came to earth *as a servant.* My mind flashed to Mark 10:45 where Christ said of Himself that He "came not to be ministered unto, but to minister," This was the "mind of Christ" I was admonished to have in me—the mind Jesus had when He came to earth from heaven.

"O Lord," I cried, "change me. Make me *only a servant.* Please give me the mind of Christ." Immediately God answered. It seemed that He reached down and scooped out of me the attitude that must have been a stench in His nostrils. And flooding over me was an overwhelming sense of only being a servant. The next morning when I started my seminar in that large church and looked out over all those people, I had the most beautiful sense of being completely *their servant*—nothing more.

Pride over a funny story could have ruined the whole seminar, but God took that story and gave me what He really wanted me (and every

Christian) to have—the mind of Christ. The mind of a servant!

There are also other references in Scripture relating to the mind of Christ and the Christian. While I was teaching my neighborhood Bible study on 1 Peter, we as a class discovered much about suffering. In chapter 4, verse 19, we found that there are those who suffer according to the will of God. And in 3:17 we discovered that "it is better, if the will of God be so, that ye suffer for well doing than for evil-doing." In 1 Peter 2:20–21 we read that when we suffer for doing well and "take it patiently, this is acceptable with God." We are called to this because "Christ also suffered for us, leaving us an example, that ye should follow His steps." I wrote in the margin of my Bible next to 1 Peter 4:1, "Lord, change *me*": "Forasmuch then as Christ hath suffered for us in the flesh, arm yourselves likewise with the same mind." As the teacher of the class, I wrote by that verse, "key verse?" Is this the key to understanding the whole of 1 Peter? Yes, we are to arm ourselves with the mind of Christ so that we can see our suffering *as* He saw His.

Also, I found it interesting, and often disconcerting, to discover the mind of Christ in the four Gospels. Most of the time His reactions were so different from what mine would have been, His attitudes so much more lofty than mine, His thoughts so far above my thoughts. But what a privilege actually to be *admonished* in Philippians 2 to have His mind *in* us.

Whenever I'm in doubt as to how God wants me to change, I am always safe in praying for the mind of Christ. So often I'm aware that my attitude, reaction, or thoughts are not Christ-like, but am not sure exactly what God wants to substitute for them. But I never ask amiss when I pray for *the mind of Christ*.

PREPARED FOR MEETINGS

When I'm preparing to speak at a seminar, retreat, or a single meeting, I sometimes have trouble feeling a burden for the people to whom I'm to minister. Struggling to put myself in the right frame of mind usually proves useless, but I have learned what does work: asking God to exchange my attitude for His.

When one meeting follows hard on the heels of another and another and another, I occasionally find lethargy setting in. Then, as I drive my car, or sit in an airplane winging my way toward a meeting, I pray, "Lord, give me a burden for these people. Please, God, take away this lethargy. Help me to feel Your burden." And God always answers that prayer. He *exchanges* my lethargy for His burden. I can feel it descend on me, almost like a weight, surrounding me and pressing from all sides. And I arrive at my destination completely prepared spiritually for the task He has given me.

I pray that same kind of prayer when I'm consumed by "the tyranny of the urgent." I find myself having to leave for a meeting in the middle of an important priority in my life. But it is time to switch gears, to let another priority have all of me. This is often difficult, but, again, I pray for God to *exchange* the urgency of one priority for what He wants me to feel for this new task. And it always works.

I could hardly face a new evening seminar series (which was about to start). In addition to being completely engrossed in writing this book, I had spent the day in holiday cleanup and washing our son's clothes for his return to college. I finally took the hour before dinner to get alone with God in my bedroom, seeking a spiritual lift for the new series. Then as I left the house for the seminar a sense of my utter inadequacy swept over me and I asked Chris to pray for me. Driving down the freeway just a few minutes later I prayed in desperation, "Lord, change me; take away this frustration. Give me joy. Make me what You want me to be at this seminar."

Almost immediately there flashed a tingle of excitement. It flooded into my whole body. I could feel it physically. Then a smile of joyous anticipation spread over my face. I pressed a little harder on the accelerator— all at once anxious to get there! God had lifted all those undesirable feelings from me and exchanged them for His attitude toward the meeting. And I faced that audience absolutely thrilled—and felt their excitement and anticipation in return.

Sometimes God answers a prayer for exchange in unexpected ways. I worked for a month preparing for a "God's Living Word" retreat (mentioned in chapter 2). Without any emotion I was typing into the message outlines the material I had culled from the three Bibles I had used devotionally since I was eighteen. Then I realized what I was doing—I was recording just dates and facts, not God's personal, dynamic speaking to me through the years. I dropped my head onto the kitchen table and fervently prayed, "O, Lord, give me the emotion I need so that this message won't be just statistics and facts. Give me the feelings You want me to have."

Before I finished praying, the phone rang. It was my former prayer partner. "My daughter's baby died last night. She has just awakened, and a flood of grief and an overwhelming sense of being unable to face life have swept over her. She wants me to talk to you. Could you say something to her?"

I wept as I recalled our Judy. And I wept as I cared about her little baby. Then I told her about one of those underlined verses I had just listed for the retreat—from Hebrews 12. I told her that God never makes a mistake, and that He must have something great in store for her and her husband to allow them such suffering. I told that grieving young mother that God was doing this "for their profit," even though they could not understand it now.

And God had *exchanged* my humdrum listing of verses and routine typing with a deep, Christ-like caring. I went to that retreat burning with the desire to impart to those women that God's Word is alive; it does have answers for right now.

God changed me in an almost violent way one night as I prepared for a retreat the next day. I had everything all in order on the pages of notes, but somehow I lacked a sense of urgency. It seemed to be just a run-of-the-mill preparation for an ordinary retreat. I realized that my heart wasn't as well prepared as my notes. So I prayed the simple but earnest prayer, "Lord, prepare *me* for tomorrow's retreat. Teach me what You want me to know and feel. Take away this feeling of nothingness."

Just then a deafening crackle resounded through our house, accompanied by a brilliant orange flash. As I sat stunned, the phone rang. My husband, calling long distance, said, "Just thought I'd let you know the tornado that was predicted for our area has moved past. You're safe now."

"Thanks a lot," I said weakly, "but our house has just been hit by lightning." I slowly hung up the phone, and sat in the total darkness. Then

I bowed my head and thanked God for protecting me. After the firemen had examined the house and told us to keep alert for possible outbreak of fire, the children and I knelt by Nancy's bed. Eleven-year-old Kurt was the first to pray, telling God we were just going to trust Him that night and go to sleep.

As I awakened the next morning safe and sound, I had a new sense of God's protection. Driving to the retreat, I found myself following a car with a bumper sticker that read "Protected by Batman." I smiled as I thought; *"I'm* protected by God!" I arrived at that retreat changed through a bolt of lightening. God had exchanged my run-of-the-mill attitude for a vital, living sense of His protection and leading in my life.

Whenever I'm feeling inadequate for a job to be done and overwhelmed by an "I-can't-do-it" feeling, I quietly commune with God. I ask Him to give me His power, His enabling in place of my inadequacy. I ask this specifically for the task that I am facing, then claim Philippians 2:13, "For it is *God who worketh in you* both to will and to do of His good pleasure." And my attitude changes. I rise to do the task, completely able to do it. God lifts my inadequacy and fills me with Himself!

EXCHANGE: GOD FOR MONEY

Years ago, in the apron-hankie-corsage era of payment for women speakers, Chris and I made a promise to God that we would never ask a fee for speaking. We told Him we would pay for baby-sitters, hairdos, and transportation out of Chris' pastor's salary—a promise we have never withdrawn, although he is no longer a pastor. Even in the early days of my prayer seminars when love offerings rarely covered expenses and prayer-letter mailings, we simply trusted God. Somehow I had always felt He would withdraw His blessings if I started serving Him for the money I might receive.

After my first book came out and my cassette tape sales increased, I was still completely detached from the income. Then people started ordering the tapes by mail. And gradually I became more and more eager to see how many orders the mailman brought. When Chris would ask what was in the mail, I would reply by telling him the number of orders I received.

Then one day as I was returning from a seminar, pushing harder and harder on the gas pedal to get home as fast as possible to see how many orders had come, God said clearly to me, "Evelyn, that attitude toward money is sin!" I was horrified. I slowed the car down and cried, "Please remove all of those thoughts and this attitude right now, Lord. O God, forgive me." And it was gone—not little by little as it had so subtly crept in; but in one sweep of His mighty cleansing hand—it was gone!

That night God had something to say to me out of His Word. As I was reading my Bible, tucking a thought in my mind to go to sleep on, a phrase in Matthew 6:24 almost jumped off the page at me: "You cannot serve both God and money" (NIV). For three nights I found myself peculiarly drawn to that same verse, from one translation to another. It was as if I wanted God to press it deeper and deeper into my very being. "I cannot serve both God and money!" Why not? God gave me that answer in the same chapter when Jesus was warning us against laying up for ourselves treasures upon earth and telling us to lay them up in heaven. Then Jesus gave the "why": "For where your treasure is, there will your heart be also" (v. 21).

God didn't say that I never could be paid for my ministry. In fact, He has some explicit instructions about the workman being worthy of his hire; but the problem lay in *where my heart was*. And He *exchanged* my wrong attitude about money for His perfect one.

MEEKNESS FOR SELF-ASSERTION

Sometimes it's a little risky to ask God to change me. I remember a pastor at a World Day of Prayer speaking on the topic, "Be careful what you pray for—God may answer your prayer." I learned the truth of this one time when I asked God to give me a meek and quiet spirit.

While preparing a banquet message on God-like characteristics in women, I was pricked by 1 Peter 3:4, where it says that we should be adorned, not with outward hairdos, ornaments, and clothes, but with "a meek and quiet spirit." Recognizing something to be desired in my steamroller personality, I prayed for five consecutive days, "Dear God, please give me a meek and quiet spirit." This was the prayer on my lips and in my heart.

I must have thought God was going to "sugarcoat" me by some supernatural process, for I was completely unprepared for the method He used. Our sixth-grade daughter had a divorced male teacher who liked to take his female pupils to a wooded retreat for outdoor education. When I refused to let our daughter go to the woods with him alone, he was furious, and came to tell me so. When I answered my doorbell, I saw him standing there with his face ashen in anger. And for the next half hour he raved and ranted at me for ruining his reputation in the community by not allowing my daughter to be alone with him in the woods, etc., etc., etc.! When he finally walked out the door, I had what I had prayed for—a meek and quiet spirit!

Yes, God had *exchanged* my personality trait for the one of His choice when I had asked Him to. But, oh, the process!

FORGIVENESS FOR GUILT

The most important exchange of all takes place when God takes our guilt and replaces it with His forgiveness, His cleansing.

While visiting in California in 1969, I heard a Sunday School teacher talk excitedly about an interesting concept in Psalm 103:12. Those were the days when we all were standing in awe of our space achievements, and she had found the concept of the Hebrew word *nasa* in that psalm. "As far as the east is from west, so far hath He removed our transgressions from us." The word "removed" conveyed the Old Testament idea of sin being separated from the sinner. And the Hebrew word *nasa* translated "forgive" meant literally to "lift away." What a picture of the dramatic blast-offs of Houston's NASA spaceships. The psalmist used the largest measurement which the earth can measure—"as far as the east is from the west," but NASA is now in the business of lifting off from Planet Earth completely!

But the comparison ends there. NASA tracks our satellites with unbelievably precise instruments and brings them back to earth again. But not God. Once He lifts them off, our sins are gone—forever. He doesn't even remember them any more! God is in the business of replacing our sins with His forgiveness.

Of course, the ultimate of this exchange of guilt for forgiveness comes when we ask God to forgive all our sins and invite Jesus to become our Lord and Savior. The greatest transformation of my life took place when I was just nine years old. At that time 2 Corinthians 5:17 became true in me: "Therefore if any man be in Christ, he is a new creation; old things are passed away; behold, all things are become new." Why is this transformation necessary? Jesus tells us clearly in John 3:18: "He that believeth on Him [God's Son] is not condemned; but he that believeth not is condemned already, because he hath not believed in the name of the only begotten Son of God."

As recorded in the Book of Mark, Jesus began His ministry in Galilee preaching *repent* and *believe*. Somehow today the emphasis is only on believing, and we tend to omit the first half of what Jesus preached (Mark 1:14–15). Then the night before He was crucified, Jesus told His disciples that He would send the Comforter who would "reprove the world of sin … because they believe not on Me" (John 16:8–9). Paul puts it so clearly in Romans 3:23: "For all have sinned, and come short of the glory of God."

But when God exchanges His forgiveness for this condemnation, the contrast is fantastic. Paul tells us that "there is therefore now no condemnation to them who are in Christ" (Rom. 8:1). Then in Colossians 1:13–14 he tells us that God has "delivered us from the power of darkness, and hath translated us into the kingdom of His dear Son; in whom we have redemption through His blood, even the forgiveness of sins." We exchange citizenship. And in Ephesians 2:1 we have the greatest exchange of all—life for death: "And you hath He [made alive], who were dead in trespasses and sins."

This exchange transforms our lifestyle according to the preceding verses. Theories and theologies are of little value if they do not produce *evidence* of their being true, if lives aren't changed.

Several years ago the churches of our city cooperated in a Teen Evangelism Crusade with Dave Wilkerson. About a thousand young people found Christ as their Savior, and the local newspaper headlines said: "Teens Say Wilkerson Visit Resulted in Changed Lives." Then they quoted some of these young people.

"It has made me a completely new person," said a sixteen-year-old boy.

"It has changed my life. I used to be a Latin Count. I used to feel like I wanted to beat up somebody all the time. I wanted to smash things."

A fifteen-year-old high school sophomore said, "I don't hate anybody any more. I feel clean inside. I get along with my mom now."

"I am no longer self-centered. Christ is the center of my life," reported a sophomore girl. "Man! If I feel low, I pray to Him—and just like that! My emptiness is gone. I love everybody."

While we were chatting with Eldridge Cleaver the other night, he looked at me and said the same thing, "There isn't anybody I don't love now." What had so dramatically changed the lifestyle of this former Black Panther fugitive? We had just come from a meeting where he told of his years of running from U.S. justice, and then of the change—beginning with his dramatic experience on the shores of the Mediterranean in southern France to the time when he asked God to forgive all his sins and Christ to be his Savior. Changed! Yes, he had *exchanged* a life of violent revolt for one of loving everybody—because God had *exchanged* in him his old nature for God's new one. It's almost as if God were in the heart transplant business. He lifts out the old heart and implants a new one.

But even after becoming a Christian there is the necessity for this exchange. John, who lived closer to Jesus on earth than any other person, included himself when he wrote in 1 John 1:8, "If we say that we have no sin, we deceive ourselves, and the truth is not in us."

Someone once said to me that we didn't have any record of the Apostle John ever sinning, "No," I replied, "except that he admitted it himself." His book of 1 John was written only to Christians, with clear directions on how "we" (John and other believers) can confess our sins so that God can forgive them (v. 1:9).

We spend so much time rationalizing and counseling in relation to what we did wrong, why we did it, what in our childhood made us do it, and on and on, that we lose sight of the fact that God says—confess it *as* sin, and I will remove your guilt. So many of our problems have an ultra-simple solution—confess what we have done or are doing as sin so that God can lift the loads of guilt. Dr. Karl Menninger, well-known psychiatrist of the Menninger Clinic in Topeka, Kansas, treats this subject of guilt powerfully in his book *Whatever Became of Sin?* (New York:

Hawthorn, 1973).

An interesting thing happens in my prayer seminars and retreats when I read a list of verses about sin from the Bible in preparation for confessing our sins to God in prayer. I watch faces change from a haughty "I-don't-have-any-sins-to-confess" expression, to a blinking in surprise, to horror, which says, "Stop, don't read any more. I can't take it."

I find it is good for me to pray through the lists of sins in God's Word. One of my favorite passages is the first eight verses of 2 Timothy 3. I stop to pray over each specific sin mentioned, asking God to reveal to me where and if that sin is in my life. I'm frequently surprised at what He tells me. But the process always works. When I confess sin as sin, God lifts the guilt from me. Exchanged!

This is a constant process in my life. God exchanging His presence for my loneliness—His power for my weakness—His healing for my illness—His hope for my despair—His peace for my anxiety—His love for my resentment—His grace for my suffering—His comfort for my sorrow. *Exchanged*—when I ask God.

7

Changed–When I Ask Others to Pray for Me

Whuh others pray for me, I change. So when I sense a need in my life I ask other people to pray. They in turn ask God to take over and do the changing, with amazing results. For over 25 years we have kept a record of all the requests that have gone through my prayer chains and groups for me, personally. Nothing has so overwhelmed me as the reviewing of these thousands of requests and answers. Whenever I read through them, I'm reminded anew that God really does change me when people pray!

BEAR YE ONE ANOTHER'S BURDENS
"Bear ye one another's burdens, and so fulfill the law of Christ" (Gal. 6:2).

Does this law of Christ concerning our responsibility to one another include *only* physical needs—food, clothing, shelter? I think not. Many of *my* needs, yes, most of my needs are not temporal. Could Christ have had in mind spiritual, emotional, and mental as well as physical needs and burdens? How I used to appreciate the casseroles that were brought in for my family when I had had surgery, a new baby, or when I was ill! But was that the *only* kind of support I needed? Was there more?

While experimenting in prayer on the theme "What Happens When Women Pray," we felt it was an indication of spiritual maturity when the women started to pray for things that could not be seen with their eyes or felt with their hands. God gave us a new dimension in our praying when we learned that there are other needs and burdens that don't have a fever, stitches, or a cast.

There are burdens that can be borne *only* in prayer.

The deepest needs I ever had while in our pastorate were not physical. Nothing temporal was lacking, but there was a desperate need in my life. The grief was so deep that I did not think I could stand before the audience to speak at an annual Christmas luncheon in one of our churches. I had shared this burden with the women of my neighborhood Bible study, and they, sensing how difficult it was going to be for me, bought tickets for the luncheon. Then they came early enough to take a place closest to the speaker's table, and sat there upholding me in prayer every minute I was speaking.

The results were dramatic. I no longer felt alone and unable to cope, because I was completely undergirded and surrounded by their love and concern. I changed because the God to whom they were praying reached down and gave me the strength, courage, and even the joy and enthusiasm I needed to share with that luncheon audience. Yes, I *changed* when they prayed for me.

Once at a Sunday School convention luncheon I had the same experience. Three of my advisory board members, sensing my special personal need that day, bought tickets and came to the luncheon. As I passed by them walking up to the speaker's table, I recognized immediately their "we're-here-praying-for-you" smiles. What a difference it made to be able to look down into their beaming faces—knowing they cared enough to spend money and time to come and help bear my burden. But the greatest part was what God did for me when they prayed. He came to that room and *changed* me with His power and strength.

Just sensing that other people are caring and praying for me is great. But the marvel is that God takes over and does what they never could do for me. Only He has the power to meet my spiritual, emotional, and mental needs. He really *changes* me when others pray.

ADMITTING OUR BURDENS

Some of our needs are obvious, especially physical ones; but many of our heaviest burdens are completely hidden to those who would pray for us—unless we share them. How can we fulfill the law of Christ in all its potential if we refuse to admit our burdens to one another?

In order to benefit to the fullest from the prayers of others, we must *admit* our needs to them. In our prayer closets it is often difficult to confess our needs to God, but we find it almost impossible to admit a weakness or need to fellow Christians. However, this is a must if we expect to experience all the support they are willing to give us.

When we first started our experimental "What Happens When Women Pray" praying, we all had a lesson to learn about praying for one another. One of our committee members had been taught to keep to herself her own needs and the needs or problems in her family, an attitude she found almost impossible to change. She was a terrific pray-er, but it stopped there. She could not admit that *she* had a need.

One day she had to leave our national committee meeting early because of a severe migraine headache. She knew that medication and rest would take several days to alleviate the problem. And she was having a baby shower at her house that night! As the time for the shower drew near, she found herself completely incapacitated. In desperation she finally decided to do what she never had done in her life: "Oh, God," she prayed, "if You want somebody to pray for me, just have them call on the phone. I won't call anyone, but if this is what You want, tell them to call me."

Almost immediately three women called her, one after another. "Hi. Just wondering if there is anything I could do for you tonight," each one said. Stunned, she broke the inhibitions that had been binding her and not once but three times said: "Please pray for me. I don't feel well. I need you to pray for me."

Admitting she had a need was hard, but God honored her honesty and humility. By the time the guests arrived, there wasn't a sign of her migraine headache or nausea. Changed!

Leaders sometimes find it especially hard to admit a need or a burden to other people. Often presidents, pastors (even pastors' wives), chairmen, and teachers feel they are to bear the burdens of other people they lead, but they find it difficult to ask those people to pray for them. Are they afraid of admitting weakness to those they lead? Are they fearful the people will think less of them as their leader if they admit a need? I think just the opposite is true. The greatest leaders surround themselves with the strongest staffs, admitting their need to be supported by them. No man is an island unto himself. Some leaders bear so many burdens unnecessarily—just because they can't admit they have a need.

One morning my phone rang as I was getting ready to speak to 1,300 people at an all-day prayer seminar. It was the president of the national organization that had invited me. She was responsible for the day's activities and was to lead all the sessions. "Evelyn, I didn't sleep well all night. And this morning I have a terrible migraine headache. I can't even eat breakfast. Would you pray for me?"

As I went to prayer I wondered what would happen to all those people and all those hours of teaching without her leadership. I prayed fervently that God would undertake and have His perfect will in her body.

When I arrived in the convention room, I inquired, "How are you feeling? How's the headache?"

"Oh," she answered a little wide-eyed, "it lifted. It's all gone!" Changed! It was because she admitted she had a need that I knew I should pray for her. And it was because she admitted her need that God was able to answer my prayer.

Just last week it was only because I let a few tears fall and admitted I had a need that my secretary put her arms around me and prayed for me.

And then I had the privilege of feeling God lift the burden that seemed so heavy—because she prayed. "O what needless pain we bear!" No human being can carry the burdens of others without having someone else bear his.

As president of our United Prayer Ministries, it is important that I admit my needs to my advisory board so that they can pray for me. Our prayer chairman calls every day for requests for my personal needs, problems, and burdens, than passes them through our prayer chains. In one two year period the women on those prayer chains prayed for 1,119 requests—over half of them for me. I could never carry on the heavy schedule I have without all that prayer. When they pray for me I *change*—change into their guided, encouraged, empowered, healed leader—because they pray! I know—because we have all the answers to their prayers dated and recorded.

One of the thrilling things about our over one-thousand-member Metro Prayer Chain in the Twin Cities area is that many Christian leaders request prayer. Admitting that they or their organization has a need activates over a thousand pray-ers—and activates God!

Even Paul, most likely the greatest Christian who ever lived, asked for prayer. In Ephesians 6:18–19 Paul asks the Christians to pray for him that utterance might be given to him, that he would be able to open his mouth boldly "to make known the mystery of the Gospel." And again in Colossians 4:3 he writes, "Praying also for us, that God would open unto us a door of utterance, to speak the mystery of Christ." In the conclusion to his first letter to the Thessalonians, he abruptly requests, "Brethren, pray for us" (5:25). And he begs the Christians in Rome to strive together with him in prayer for his deliverance from the unbelievers in Judea, that his service might be accepted by the saints in Jerusalem, that he might come to them with joy by the will of God and might with them be refreshed (Rom. 15:31–31). Paul was not ashamed to *admit* his numerous needs or to ask Christians to pray *for* him.

Did Paul really expect to find himself and circumstances around him *changed* because people prayed for him? Why else would he have asked them to pray?

DEPENDENCE

Perhaps one of the reasons we find admitting our needs to other people so difficult is that by doing so we are admitting we are dependent—dependent upon God and upon other people. We are a generation of "I-can-do-it-myself-God" Christians.

Whether we want to admit it or not, we are dependent on other prayers. In Matthew 9:38 Jesus said, "Pray ye, therefore, the Lord of the harvest, that He will send forth laborers into His harvest." Am I a laborer because someone, sometime, somewhere, obeyed Jesus' command and prayed that God would send forth a laborer to the field in which I'm working? This is a humbling thought, and removes all the ego and pride about *my* ministry, *my* calling. Because somebody prayed, did I CHANGE into God's laborer?

If Paul was dependent on his friends to pray for utterance to be given to him, how much of *my* having utterance in my ministry is because somebody, or many people prayed for me? How dependent am I on other people's prayers for enabling me to teach my prayer seminars? In Ephesians 6:18–19 Paul asked prayer for utterance for himself and all saints—me! How much did I CHANGE because of them?

Frequently we don't know we have been depending on the prayers of others until we see the results. When Peter was in prison (Acts 12:5–19), he may not have been aware that "prayer was made without ceasing of the church unto God for him" (v. 5). Perhaps not until the chains fell off his hands, and he walked out of prison as the iron gate opened did he realize that God must be answering prayer. Or was it when the believers finally opened the door of the house and he saw them "praying without ceasing," that he realized why he was freed?

Scripture tells us in 1 Timothy 2:2 that we are to pray "for kings and for all that are in authority." So, whether or not they know it, leaders are dependent upon the prayers of those who obey this command. When God reaches down and *changes* kings and those in authority and the circumstances surrounding them even without their knowledge, they are dependent upon the prayers.

Or when we experience relief from some physical problem before it runs its natural course, it may well be that our fellow Christians are obeying the admonition in James to "pray one for another that ye may be healed" (5:16). When we are miraculously *changed* physically, how dependent were we on God's faithful pray-ers?

How much do I change because other people pray for me? Only eternity will tell. Only God knows who activated the process of change that takes place in me.

SPIRITUAL WARFARE

Since the Father and the Son are One, I'm constantly amazed that God had need of Jesus' prayers on behalf of others. Jesus must have known that this is the process God uses, yes, expects, when others have needs, for in His High-Priestly Prayer He prayed for His followers and for us.

And in that prayer Jesus prayed that the Father would keep them and us "from the evil one" (John 17:15). He didn't pray that God would remove us from the evil one's domain, Planet Earth; just that God would deliver us from him. Because Christ is our Example in all things, we too should pray this prayer for other believers.

Jesus also practiced this kind of prayer specifically when Satan wanted to sift Peter. He said, "But I have prayed for thee, that thy faith fail not" (Luke 22:32). But in spite of Jesus' prayer for him, cocky Peter—cocksure he wouldn't fall into the enemy's trap before the cock would crow—denied his Lord. Jesus knew the importance of praying for those who are tempted by Satan.

When Dr. Kurt Koch was in our Twin Cities awhile ago to lead seminars in opposition to the occult explosion in America, he begged us to pray for him. He had just canceled a series of seminars in New York and had to be flown back to Germany because of a severe physical problem that he attributed to the lack of prayer on the part of Christians in America as he spoke on this perilous subject. "Americans don't know how to pray in this battle," he told us. He pled with us to follow faithfully, fervently, Christ's example in His High-Priestly Prayer. Dr. Koch had changed—for the worse—because of lack of prayer.

In Ephesians 6:18–19 Paul's exhortation is to pray always for all saints and for himself. Prayer is part of the armor that Christians are to use in the battle against spiritual wickedness—the realm of Satan. Once

I bravely tackled a Bible study subject on "Ephesians in the Light of the Spirit World" (fools rush in where angels fear to tread), and experienced unusual resistance from the enemy. But in the margin of my Bible next to Ephesians 6:18, I wrote: "2/29/72. Great power first Bible study. Host of people praying. I could *feel* power. Never felt more when speaking." I had *changed* from an intimidated and harassed woman trying to prepare a Bible study that was a threat to Satan—*changed* into an empowered teacher. Because they prayed!

Tell Me Your Secret

Many times after teaching my whole seminar on prayer in one day (five and one-half to six hours of lecturing), a pastor or priest will come to me and say, "Tell me your secret. How can you 'speak to convince' so many hours in a row? When I finish speaking for one or two hours on a Sunday morning, I'm exhausted. I'm completely overcome with fatigue. What's your secret?"

"I do have a secret," I tell them honestly. "It's my prayer support. It is all the women who so faithfully pray for me."

Yes, I do have a secret. One January 4th, after writing every spare minute during the holidays and then teaching a large first-of-the-year prayer seminar the night before, I awoke too exhausted to get out of bed. This was a rare occurrence in my life for I'm an early riser; but, as Chris put a towel over my eyes, I thanked God silently that he was going to a breakfast meeting that morning. Then, suddenly, surging through my body was strength, eagerness to get going on the day the Lord had given me. I was *changed*—there was a complete transformation. What had happened? The prayer chain members one by one were arising and having their quiet times with the Lord—and praying for me!

Not long ago I became aware that at exactly 6 o'clock every morning I felt a surge of God's power. Questioning the recurrence at the same time every morning, I casually mentioned it to one of the women who had been sending through the prayer requests for one of my prayer chains. I could almost see her blushing in modest humility over the phone as she stammered, "That's the time I pray for you every morning." I could feel the change come over me—as she prayed!

One day last fall this prayer request went through the chain for me: "Evelyn in desperate need of strength." Then the record of the answer made a couple of days later read, "Over 3,000 people attended her workshops. Ev stood and talked fourteen hours one evening and next day. Experienced Isaiah 40:31."

Last November 23 I asked the prayer chains to pray because I was already tired and facing an all-day prayer seminar. I just reread the astounding answer recorded in our files "Ev gained momentum as the day progressed." *Changed?* Yes!

When others pray for me, God, the omnipotent God of heaven and earth, reaches down and changes me—because they pray—because they are willing to fulfill the law of Christ by bearing my burdens.

FOR ONE ANOTHER

But the greatest joy in prayer is not just being prayed for, but bearing one another's burdens. Sprinkled all through our advisory board and other prayer chains are the personal and family needs of our members. What a privilege to pray for one daughter in distress, and then a year later to be praying for her as she leads a Bible study at Urbana—changed! And after praying for a member's arthritis surgery, to be told of the dramatic, almost painless success of the operation, or to pray for a Christian college professor's son from another state who was on alcohol and marijuana, and then to receive a thrilling letter that there is victory—changed! There was the mother with a stroke, the woman with the migraine headaches, the opening of a new Christian bookstore, and the responsibilities of the "Here's Life" city-wide prayer chairman—circumstances and people— all changed according to God's will for them because we prayed!

Yes, it's hard to admit we need to be changed and it's very hard to admit to other Christians that we need them to pray so that God will change us. Yes, it is a humbling process, but it's so rewarding. When others pray for me—I change!

8

Changed—When I Pray for Others

*T*he fourteen months of my "Lord, change me" silence didn't mean I gave up my intercessory prayer life learned so diligently during the previous six months. In fact, the paradox of this period was that it was at the peak of our telephone prayer chain ministry. But when I started praying, "Lord, change me," an unexpected change took place in my intercessory prayer life. As I prayed for Jan, I was praying for God's will, not mine, for her. Instead of superimposing my will upon her, I found myself praying for God to change her the way *He* wanted her to be changed. In the struggle of that long quiet period I learned a profound secret: *release*.

RELEASED

Releasing, I was to discover, was giving back to God something He had given me. Yes, Jan was a gift from Him. "Lo, children are an heritage of the Lord," we are told in Psalm 127:3. Though Chris and I had given her to the Lord before she was born (as we have all our children), this situation was different. It meant literal releasing—Jan was of legal age. I almost felt like Hannah as she gave her weaned child, Samuel, to the Lord. It was similar to what I experienced when the doctors told us that our Judy could not live. As I prayed for her that night, it wasn't until I *released* her to God for *His* will to be done that the battle was over. Not the grief—but the battle was over. I changed that night. I had released her to God!

Even the releasing of our children to God's care every day as they left for kindergarten and continued on through high school taught me so much about this process. Releasing them to God's protection and guidance when I couldn't accompany them to school, when my empty hand ached to hold theirs in this big, frightening world, was preparing me for the actual releasing that would take place in the future.

Releasing Jan to God intensified my prayers for her. So often what I do for a child is too little, too late. But God always does everything in the right way, at the right time. What I want for a child may be dictated by selfish motives—the best-paying job, the place of greatest honor, the highest grade, the biggest house—things the world equates with success. But not God. He always wants for them what will teach them the most, and that which will make them the finest gold.

I'll never forget what a mother of several teenagers once said to me. "I'm not sending my kids to a Christian college only to have them go to a foreign mission field, as my brother did, and leave *me* all alone in my old age." I see this process of releasing take place in our prayer seminars so frequently. The most life-changing session we have is the one where we learn to pray in God's will. At the close we think of the most important thing in the whole world to us, and then give it to God in prayer. This is the point at which we release to God our right to that person or thing which is more important to us than anything else at the time.

While conducting a prayer seminar in a friend's church in California,

I watched an astounding change take place in her pastor. His wife is a beautiful, talented, and charming hostess—but she is gravely ill with cancer. Throughout their pastorate, she has been his supportive co-worker. When I arrived for that seminar, I was introduced to the most heartbroken pastor I ever have seen. But a miracle happened while we were praying in our small groups after studying how to pray in God's will. That pastor released his wife to God for *His* will for her—not his own. As he came to the pulpit to close the session in prayer, I couldn't believe my eyes. "Is that man radiating?" I whispered to my friend. His face seemed literally to glow as he smiled at his congregation and told them what had happened. "He's radiating!" she whispered back. The wife hadn't changed—but the one who released her had!

Talking with a woman at a seminar yesterday, I listened as she told me that her husband who had had surgery several times had been told by his doctors that he could not get well. It was only a matter of time. She told me of her days and weeks of struggle and rebellion against God and of her refusal to give him up. "But," she said, "the miracle came when I released him to God. *I* was the one who changed. The battle was over." Then she added, "Oh, by the way, he's the gentleman you were just talking to over there. He's completely cured." But his recovery wasn't the only miracle. The miracle that happened when she released him to God was just as life-changing.

Perhaps the most difficult time to release our "human possessions" to God is when He is disciplining them. How we love to protect our children, our spouses, and our loved ones from God's discipline. At a recent retreat I was counseling a woman whose pastor husband had been having an affair with another woman. Having been discovered, he was in deep depression. She told me that she was asking God not to deal with him any more because she was afraid he wouldn't be able to take it. She was trying to protect him from God! I told her that the only hope for her husband was for her to *release* him to God, the only One who could convict him of the *sin* of his actions. Then her husband could assume his responsibility before God and confess his sin. "Stop trying to play God," I told her.

The first time Jan faced exams at college after I released her to God,

I remember how different were my prayers for her: "God, don't necessarily give her all A's, but teach her everything she needs to know this first year of college." I remember Jan jokingly (but deep down inside, seriously) telling her friend not to have her mother pray for her. "She'll pray you right out of all A's." Well, I really wasn't the one who caused the one "B" that first semester, but in a way I felt responsible, for I *had* prayed that God would teach her *everything* He knew she needed to know. And He obviously knew (as I was to learn later) that there are more important things than all A's earned immediately upon entering college. Of course, all A's were as exciting to us as to her, but I had submitted to His will. I had released her for Him—not me—to teach her.

A missionary used half a box of Kleenex as she tearfully told me her story at a retreat. God had called her and her husband back to the United States and had given them a pastorate. She told me between her sobs that both she and her husband were absolutely positive that it was God's will that they were here. "But," she sobbed, "people won't release us. 'Once a missionary, always a missionary,' they say. It's the people *who pray for us* who won't give us to God for *His* will in our lives. They want to tell God where we should be serving Him."

How we love to play God in other people's lives—especially in those for whom we are diligently praying. But God wants *us* to change—to release them to Him for His will. Jesus taught us to pray for them that way in the Lord's Prayer in Matthew 6:9–10 when He said, "After this manner ... pray ye ... *Thy* will be done in earth, as it is in heaven."

When I was president of our Bethel College's faculty wives' association, we planned a "Lord, change me" retreat. While announcing it, I explained to the college and seminary faculty and staff husbands that we wives were going to draw apart at a retreat center and let God tell us from His Word what He wanted changed in us. "I don't want my wife changed. I like her the way she is," quipped one professor.

I held my silence, but how I wanted to say to him, "But does *God* like her the way she is?" There's a difference!

I praise and thank God for a husband who has released me to God for *His* will in my life. How beautiful our marriage relationship is since Chris is interested not in what *he* wants for me, selfishly and personally, but in what *God* wants for me. Yes, it involves sacrifice to release a loved one to God, but the beauty of that submissive, changed life is great to behold.

RELEASING OUR SPIRITUAL CHILDREN

We often have a tendency too to be over-possessive of our "spiritual children." I had been telling my telephone prayer chain chairman about talking long distance to a woman who had led many people to the Lord and was now physically and emotionally exhausted from trying to keep them all afloat. As she was discipling, mothering, and coaching, she found herself collapsing under the strain.

"Release them to God," I had advised her, "and let Him give them back to you one at a time for only those things He wants you to do for them."

The next day my prayer chairman called and said, "I took personally the advice you gave the other person over the phone. I suddenly realized that I was spoon-feeding my neighbors, feeling totally responsible for all of them all of the time. And I too am under a doctor's care, not able to take the strain any longer, so I just *released* these neighbors to God. I won't stop being concerned. I won't stop discipling and nurturing them; I'll only stop playing God."

Babies never learn to walk if adults refuse to let go of their hands. New Christians never learn to walk if we insist on carrying them. Although discipling is a necessary part of helping those whom we have introduced to Christ, there comes a time when we must *release* them to fly by themselves with God.

When we release our right to our own will for our "human possessions," we change—becoming submissive to God's will rather than demanding our will for them. But there is an added bonus in this process I had not counted on, and certainly had not sought. While God was changing me, He was also teaching me the effectiveness of His changing others for whom I was only praying, not "preaching at."

I saw myself in a new role—changed! On intercessor's knees, I found it much more effective to talk to God about things in their lives of which I didn't approve and letting *Him* handle them. Gradually I learned that there is more power in praying for people than in preaching at people, especially when I have released them for God to answer my prayers in any way He desires.

CHANGE—WHILE I PRAYED

One of the greatest privileges for mortals on this planet is to be able to come boldly to the throne of grace (Heb. 4:16). When I exercise this privilege, I change. I see the worth God has placed upon me when He allows, yes, invites me to come into His presence in prayer. I, a mere mortal, have the overwhelming joy of bringing those for whom I'm concerned right to the throne of the God of the universe. I have the attention of the omniscient, omnipotent, omnipresent God—and this changes me!

The reason we are continuing our twenty-four-hour "Here's Life" prayer chains in our churches now that our "I Found It" saturation is over is that many pray-ers have told us they don't want to give up the privilege of intercession. The joy they experienced on their twenty-four-hour-prayer-chains, even when their hour to pray was scheduled in the middle of the night, was tremendous, they told us. The privilege of having access to God in that very special way is something many are not willing to give up.

Also, while I am praying for others, I am fulfilling the admonition of Colossians 3:1–2, "If ye, then, be risen with Christ, seek those things which are above, where Christ sitteth on the right hand of God. Set your affection on things above, not on things on the earth." Keeping my mind in the heavenlies, being transported mentally into the presence of God the Father and Christ His Son, changes me. When Jesus took Peter, James, and John up into a mountain to pray, we read that "as He [Jesus] prayed, the appearance of His countenance was altered" (Luke 9:28, RSV). It was while *He prayed* that Jesus' appearance changed. Matthew tells us that His face "did shine as the sun" (Matt. 17:2). And as I pray, God changes me. While I am directly associating with my holy God, high and lifted up, I become more Christ-like, more conformed to His image.

We read in the Book of Acts that two of these same men were brought as prisoners before the rulers, elders, scribes, and all the kindred of the high priest. And when they saw Peter and John, "they took note of them that these men had been with Jesus" (Acts 4:13, NIV). We teach our children they will be like the people with whom they associate. Is there really something different about us when we have been with Jesus? Yes, we really are changed—so much so that even *our* enemies also can tell the difference.

SOMEBODY NEEDS ME

Inherent in each human being is the need to be needed. It gives us a sense of self-worth, a zest for life, and a reason for living.

In our prayer seminars we discover the worth of ourselves as we practice intercessory prayer. As the urgent and often heartbreaking prayer requests are handed in, pray-ers find—many for the first time—that *someone* really does need them, and their prayers.

Corrie ten Boom told me that when she was five years old and had just received Christ as her Savior, her mother said to her, "Corrie, now you are an intercessor." And she found that the people living around her home needed her prayers. What a great way for a little child to find her self-worth!

Trying to motivate and instill a sense of self-worth in teenagers at a 5-week prayer seminar proved to be a difficult experience. These were 200 members of a confirmation class who, along with a church full of adults, were learning to pray. But their presence was not voluntary, and the paper wads, bubble gum and paper airplanes displayed on the first night showed me what they thought of themselves as pray-ers.

At the second session one of them came to me and said she had a prayer request. "My ten-year-old sister cannot hear," she said. Fearing I'd never be able to motivate them if God chose to answer some way other then healing her sister, I decided on a plan. I challenged those 200 teenagers by giving *them* the request. I told them it was their responsibility, *theirs* to do whatever they chose with it. I held my breath all that next week waiting for the outcome. At the next session my fears proved to be in vain. I found myself surrounded by a whole gang of the girl's teenage friends as she excitedly announced, "Guess what happened to my sister?" I waited with bated breath. "She can now hear without her hearing aid!" Those 200 teenagers had found the worth of themselves to someone in need.

After the last session of that prayer seminar, the pastor's wife came to me with tears in her eyes. "Do you remember the boy who was shooting paper airplanes and paper wads that first night? (How could I forget him?) Do you know what he just prayed in our little group? He prayed, 'Dear God, please teach my dad what You've just taught me!'" Oh, yes, we change when we discover we are needed.

GOD NEEDS ME

Some of the greatest untapped potentials in our churches are our infirm members. Many of them were great spiritual giants while their bodies were still strong, but now that disease or old age has forced them to become inactive for God as they are confined to their rocking chairs, wheel chairs, or beds, their spirits often become as shriveled as their bodies. But I've discovered something exciting in our prayer seminars. Relatives and friends frequently bring these people to a seminar, and occasionally they even come by bus from nursing homes. I challenge these infirm Christians that God *still* needs them, and I tell them that they can once again exercise as much and perhaps more spiritual power then they did before. I love to watch these bypassed citizens of God's kingdom unfold like a rose as they rediscover that God needs them.

While experimenting in our "What Happens When Women Pray" praying, we assigned these people as prayer support for our neighborhood Bible studies. What a release of God's power and what changed results we saw in the Bible studies as the teachers and hostesses kept their "pray-er" up to date on all the needs and problems of the class!

One of our outstanding primary department teachers became physically unable to teach her class. Home-baked cookies and deep personal concern for every pupil had made her a teacher who was deeply loved. But after having to relinquish her class, she launched a new project from her hospital bed and home confinement—she spent the Sunday School hour praying by name for each pupil in her department and for the teachers and superintendent. Almost immediately the other teachers began to report that amazing changes were taking place in that department. Discipline problems went almost to zero. Did God *need* her more in that capacity than teaching her class of primary boys and girls? Evidently. Yes, God had allowed her to be changed from an active person to an inactive person, but instead of folding up in her confinement, she was changed into a powerful intercessor.

While I was conducting a prayer seminar in a large Southern city, a psychiatrist told me, "You know, my profession isn't known for its cures, but I am discovering something interesting. I've been a Christian for only two years, but I've started to pray for my patients—deep, fervent prayer. And," she continued excitedly, "I'm finding that those for whom I pray," she took a deep breath before finishing, "actually get well." And *she* was a changed psychiatrist, overawed that God was actually doing something for her patients when she prayed for them.

When we first started experimenting in prayer, the thing that changed the original "eight gripers" into motivated and faithful pray-ers was the discovery that God actually needed them. And I have found this to be true through the years as I have taught thousands to pray. Watching people change from skeptical doubters to exuberant pray-ers, when they discover God is using *them*, is a constant thrill to me. A pastor's wife told me this morning that sometimes she prays for a need that only she knows about and for which no one else is praying, then *knows* it is *her* prayer that God is answering. The startling discovery that God is using *us* does change our sense of self-worth. We are changed—needed—people. And that makes us joyful people!

Sweet and Bitter Water

When I become an intercessor, praying *for* other people, I find the truth of James 3:11–12 becoming evident in my life. I find it is impossible for two attitudes to be in me at the same time. "Doth a fountain send forth at the same place sweet water and bitter? Can the fig tree, my brethren, bear olive berries? either a vine, figs? So can no fountain yield both salt water and fresh."

When I pray for others, it takes my mind off my trivial or perhaps very real complaints. There is always someone worse off than I, and when I go into deep intercessory prayer for that person I change from a self-centered complainer into a person with genuine concern and love for that one for whom I pray. Somehow I can't concentrate on myself and pray out of love for others at the same time.

CHANGED—WHEN I PRAY FOR OTHERS

I find too that it is impossible to pray for and gossip about a person at the same time. One of the great results of a telephone prayer chain is that the pray-ers stop gossiping about other people's troubles when they start praying about them. Also, "roast pastor" is no longer a Sunday dinner main dish when we really start praying for him.

And I can't thank God for all the good things about a person and be filled with accusations at the same time. Somehow those two diametrically opposed attitudes can't be expressed simultaneously. This is one of the subtle results of thanking God for all our acquaintances—especially our enemies. During the process, *we* change.

I also find it impossible to pray for and be angry with a person at the same time. Could Christ have had something more in mind than the persons for whom He commanded us to pray, when He said in Matthew 5:44, "Pray for them which despitefully use you"? Could one of the results of praying for those who despitefully use us be that we, the pray-ers, are changed *as* we pray for them? But in order to effect this change, our prayers must be genuine. We cannot utter a few sweet words in prayer while the bitterness remains deep down inside. No, real prayer is the overflow of the heart.

The first step to take to insure the sweetness within is to forgive the person who has despitefully used us. It is at this point that we are changed on the inside. We are changed *when* we forgive others.

A retired missionary came to me yesterday and told me that the women in her church were studying *What Happens When Women Pray*. Tears came into her eyes as she said, "The crisis chapter of that book is the one about forgiving others. One thing after another is cleared up between people when they forgive each other. It is making such a difference in our church."

A woman attending a seminar in a Minneapolis suburb wanted me to play "Ann Landers" and advise her on how to tell her mother-in-law off. I asked her to wait until the next week when we would study how to handle such situations. The following session included the formula for forgiving others—and she prayed through! The next week she came bouncing into the seminar a completely changed person. A sweet spirit had replaced her acute agitation; a smile had replaced her troubled countenance. I never met the mother-in-law. Whether she continued to be her evidently rather miserable self or was changed as her daughter-in-law's attitude toward her changed, I will most likely never know. But this I do know—a radical change took place in the one who forgave her.

Two college girls burst into the dean of women's office after I finished teaching their prayer-week session on forgiving others. "I'm free. I'm free!" Although I didn't have the foggiest idea who had been involved or what the problem was, the dean of women nodded and smiled an understanding smile. Something had been solved on that Christian campus. And the one doing the forgiving had the privilege of being changed. Free!

A very agitated woman from Germany came to the former Nazi Hansi ("The Girl who Loved the Swastika") telling her she could not stand her mother. They got along all right as long as the Atlantic Ocean was between them, but she had just received word that her mother was coming to America from Germany!

"Why don't you come to the prayer seminar at my church tomorrow night?" Hansi suggested. She came—and we just happened to be having the lesson on forgiving others. As the rows of people turned to pray together, Hansi found herself facing this angry woman. After having chosen her mother as the one person to forgive during prayer time, she looked up at Hansi and said, "Oh, now my mother can come from Germany!" Who changed? The mother? No, *when* she forgave her mother, *she* changed!

God wisely gave that little formula in 2 Corinthians 2:5–11 to those who have been grieved. We somehow feel that the person who grieved us is the one who needs to change, but God wisely places the responsibility on us when we have been despitefully used. There isn't anything in that formula that tells the person who has caused the grief what to do, but only what we, the grieved ones, must do. God knew all along that when we forgive someone and pray for him out of real love, we change.

Yes, when I pray for others, I change! *My* priorities, *my* rights, *my* attitudes, all change *as* I pray for other people.

SECTION III

Make Sure It Is the Lord Doing the Changing

9

Source of Wisdom No. 1— My Sensual Self

"The way of a fool is right in his own eyes ... "

PROVERBS 12:15

Now that we've looked into the methods God uses to change us, the haunting question arises: How can I be absolutely sure it is the Lord who is changing me? How can I know that my lifestyle, the sum total of all my wisdom put into action, is really from Him?

God showed me the fact that the Book of James mentions four sources of wisdom from which I can obtain knowledge that will change me. These four are constantly vying for my lifestyle; and I discovered that only one of them is God. Only one of the four is a trustworthy source of direction for the changes in my life. The other three are mentioned in James 3:15: "This wisdom descendeth not from above, but is *earthly* [from other people], *sensual* [from within our sensual selves], *demo-*

niacal [from demons]" (SCO).

Is there any way, then, that I can test the source of wisdom that is producing my lifestyle? James says the proof is in *what it produces*: "The wisdom that is from above [from the Lord] is first pure, then peaceable, gentle, and easy to be entreated, full of mercy and good fruits, without partiality, and without hypocrisy" (3:17). This is in contrast to what the other three sources produce: "But if ye have bitter envying and strife in your hearts, glory not, and lie not against the truth. This wisdom descendeth not from above, but is earthly, sensual, demonical. For where envying and strife are, there is confusion and every evil work" (vv. 14–16, SCO).

Sometimes it is difficult to discern which source of wisdom has produced a change in me. It is possible for the sources other than God to produce temporary satisfaction with the good life, but the end result will always be the opposite of what God wants to produce in me. Superficial happiness may be produced from one of the other sources of wisdom, but there will be an absence of real joy and peace down deep within me.

I discovered this frightening fact while reading devotionally in James 3 one Sunday morning several years ago. Anger over something a relative had said to me nine years before suddenly welled up within me. I had forgiven and been forgiven at that time, so why this recurrence of these feelings? As I read this portion of Scripture I knew God's answer: that attitude was not from Him! Horrified, I noted the other three sources of wisdom, and then realized that wisdom from God would not produce the anger I was experiencing. It had to be from one of the other sources.

In these final chapters I will discuss these four possible sources of wisdom which can produce changes that collectively result in my lifestyle.

MY SENSUAL SELF

One of the sources from which I can receive wisdom is my own sensual self—*the part of me that is controlled by my senses*. It is the natural man that Paul struggled with in Romans 7. "For I know that in me (that is, in my flesh) dwelleth no good thing" (v. 18). "So then with the mind I myself serve the law of God; but with the flesh the law of sin" (v. 25b).

Christ, on one occasion when "He had called all the people to Him,"

painted a word picture of the human heart that was far from compli-
mentary: "For from within, out of the heart of men, proceed evil
thoughts, adulteries, fornications, murders, thefts, covetousness, wickedness, deceit, lasciviousness, an evil eye, blasphemy, pride, foolishness: All
these evil things come from within us, and defile the man" (Mark
7:21–23). James wrote about a source of sin that was within us: "But every
man is tempted, when he is drawn away of his own lust, and enticed"
(James 1:14). And Jeremiah lamented, "The heart is deceitful above all
things, and desperately wicked: who can know it?" (Jeremiah 17:9).

DECEIVING MYSELF

After reading what the Bible says about my sensual self, I'm appalled that
I can deceive myself into thinking I know what direction my changing
should take. A profound proverb says, "The way of a fool is right in his
own eyes" (Prov. 12:15). And in Romans, Paul describes those who "when
they knew God … became vain in their imaginations, and their foolish
heart was darkened. Professing themselves to be wise, they became
fools" (1:21–22). Because "they did not like to retain God in their
knowledge, God gave them over to a reprobate mind, to do those
things which are not convenient; Being filled with all unrighteousness,
fornication, wickedness, covetousness, maliciousness; full of envy, mur-
der, debate, deceit, malignity; whispers, backbiters, haters of God,
despiteful, proud, boasters, inventors of evil things, disobedient to parents, without understanding, covenant-breakers, without natural affection, implacable, unmerciful" (1:28–31). Are all these things really the
end results of rationalizing and following my own feelings and senses?
The possibility of any of these consequences being a part of my life sends
me scurrying to God's Word for His direction on how to change.

What can I do about this sensuous self? God has some good advice for
me. In Ephesians I read that "henceforth (from now on, since I am in
Christ Jesus), I am not to walk as other Gentiles walk, *in the vanity of
their mind*". … But I am to "put off concerning the former [manner of
life] the old man, which is corrupt according to the deceitful lusts; and
be *renewed in the spirit of* [my] *mind*" (4:17ff). God wants to change me,
wants to give me wisdom from Him that will produce the opposite of

these sins of the flesh.

So in prayer I cry to God with the psalmist, "Search me, O God, and know my heart; try me, and know my thoughts; and see if there be any wicked way in me, and lead me in the way everlasting" (Ps. 139:23–24). "Don't let me be changed by what *I* think or feel. Give me the wisdom for changing that is from You."

"I THINKS"

What I think really isn't very impressive according to God's Word. There is only one Truth, and that is from God Himself. The only absolute truth on which we can depend for the right kind of changes in our lives is found only in God's Word "Sanctify them in truth. Thy word is truth" (John 17:17).

We have a rule about this at our house. Last summer I overheard two of our children discussing it: "Mother always said truth is truth. It doesn't matter if you believe it or not. And not believing it has nothing to do with the fact that it is truth, and it will not change from being truth just because we choose not to believe it."

Yes, whether or not I agree with something has nothing to do with whether or not it is true. My "I think" about a subject neither negates it nor insures its being true.

But we are so prone to believe our "I thinks" are very important. Many times what is billed as a Bible study turns out to be an exchange of our "I thinks." We read the Scripture portion and, using it as a springboard, dive immediately into the inner pool of our "I thinks" and begin a discussion of whatever comes to our minds. When we are finished telling what we think about the subject, other class members usually retain what they think, and I keep what I think. It may have been a great discussion, but no one acquired any new truth from God's Word.

A rule for Bible study that assures us of getting wisdom from the only worthy Source, God Himself, is that we don't discuss anything that is not answered in the portion of Scripture being studied on a given day. The teacher, and hopefully the pupils, will have studied the actual meaning of text, and the answers no longer will be the participants' "I think" but God's Word. Then we know that the changes we make in our lives based on that lesson are not from the "I thinks" of people but from God Himself.

I was conducting a retreat in an Eastern state, and on the Saturday morning we were to practice reading God's Word individually until He pointed out something in our lives that needed changing. The hearts of those women had really been prepared during their cabin devotions the night before. Someone had listed some excellent questions on "How do you react when … ?" The object was to discover if one's reactions were Christ-like or not. But something went wrong. I sat in the corner quietly listening to their discussions. They became more and more heated as the women exchanged their "I thinks" —disagreeing, ignoring, and vying for the floor. The next morning I asked how many could honestly say they learned something during the devotions the night before, and not one single hand was raised. But in another way they had learned a tremendous lesson, and were eager to listen to God that morning.

A professor at one of our large seminaries told me that the school was changing its teaching policy because the students had requested less group-interaction sessions and more teacher sessions. These students felt that there was far too much to learn to warrant so much time being spent in sharing their "I thinks."

However, this does not mean that we cannot learn from each other. Sharing can be a profitable source of wisdom—if the wisdom shared is from a worthy source. If the source has been what God taught that person, then the sharing will be profitable indeed. If the teacher says, "I think," the pupil well may respond, "So what?" And the same holds true when the teacher verbalizes his or her own feelings. They are not grounds for expecting or demanding change in the pupil. But when the teacher's source of wisdom has come from God or those who also learned from God, then the "I think" becomes positive wisdom.

This too is why we do not approach Bible reading or study with our minds full of our own preconceived ideas.

Asking God to remove preconceived ideas *before* writing would have helped the author of a widespread women's study to interpret and teach Genesis 1:26 and 28 correctly. Approaching the Scriptures with the preconceived idea that God gave the male the roles of dominion and procreation had blinded the author's eyes to the pronouns being plural, not singular ("them," and not "him"). An accurate reading gives male and female equal dominion and procreation roles and thus negates the basis of the thesis of the study. And looking up the meaning of the words "Adam" and "man" in this portion in a good Bible word study would have revealed that both words are plural—also disproving the preconceived thesis.

Sometimes our "I thinks" are produced by inadequate Bible study. A young male student assailed me after I had led a prayer seminar in his college prayer week. After teaching them, I had asked the student body to stand and make small groups for prayer. "You know very well," he exploded at me, "that nowhere in the Bible does it tell women to tell men to do anything."

"Oh," I said in surprise, "except Jesus and the angels on Resurrection morning both told the women to go and tell the men—not only that Jesus was not dead—but to go to Galilee where He said they would see Him too."

His preconceived "I think" had robbed him of seeing the truth about how the most important fact in the history of mankind—He is risen!—was revealed and then relayed to Christ's male followers.

*   *   *

A lawyer in a class I was teaching in the Book of Mark came to me after class and objected, "Why are you teaching all this about Satan and demons? You know very well there's no such thing."

In our verse-by-verse study, I was not choosing topics but simply teaching whatever subject was covered in the text, and the first few lessons had all included some encounter with these beings.

I replied, "You are a very intelligent man. I want you to do something for me. Take at least the Book of Mark, and all four Gospels if you have time, and write down as if you were preparing a legal case every time Satan or demons are mentioned, who said what, how each reacted, who was victorious, etc. When you have finished, tell me your decision about the reality of these things and I promise to abide by your decision as to whether or not I will teach about them."

By the next Friday a note had arrived in my mail box: "Dear Mrs. Chris: Please forgive me. I only thought I knew what the Bible said about that subject. I hadn't really read it."

*   *   *

Sometimes we take a perfectly good word from the Bible (such as "chastisement," "suffering," "submission," "healing," "God's justice"), dive immediately into our pool of "I thinks" and weave them subtly and securely around that word, leaving the impression that all of our "I thinks" about the word actually were included in the scriptural meaning of the word.

Also it is important to base a theological premise on *all* the Scriptures dealing with the subject and not from our ideas from just one Scripture portion. It is easy to believe that prayer should be made only in a closet, only holding up holy hands, only kneeling down, or only lying in bed when we take what that particular Scripture has to say about prayer. But, in order to get a true, complete picture of scriptural prayer, all Scripture on that subject must be viewed collectively.

So also it is easy to get a lopsided view of women staying home and being keepers at home, whereas many of Paul's co-workers were women. Priscilla traveled with Paul (Acts 18:18), taught Apollos, and the four Gospels abound with women traveling with Jesus. And these same women made up a large part of the 120 waiting and praying together with the men after the ascension of Christ back to heaven (Acts 1:14). Then we next see them still with the apostles and other men at Pentecost with the Holy Spirit falling on *all* who were in that prayer group, and *all* of them speaking to the visitors in Jerusalem from many different countries—in their native tongues. Peter explained this phenomenon not as *being* drunkenness, as was supposed, but as the fulfilling of Joel's prophecy: "But this is that which was spoken by the Prophet, Joel; 'And it shall come to pass in the last days,' saith God, 'I will pour out of My Spirit upon all flesh: and your sons and your *daughters* shall prophesy, and your young men shall see visions, and your old men shall dream dreams: And on My servants and on My handmaidens I will pour out in those days of My Spirit; and they shall prophesy'" (Acts 2:16–18).

Many of these verses, you may have noticed, have to do with the role of women within the church. Lest someone suspect that I as a woman am anxious to advance my own "I think," I will assure you that the issues growing out of these passages are the ones that have been coming up week after week in the prayer seminars around the country.

Many women have shared with me how they have allowed someone's "I think" to thwart their usefulness and to render them almost subhuman. Bookstores are filled with women's books, some advocating total submission to men, others suggesting ways a wife may manipulate her husband to "keep him happy and save the marriage"; still others suggest that Christians abandon male-female roles altogether.

Few topics of late have been so popular—or so polarizing. Because so many men and women are being hurt because of a misunderstanding of male-female roles in the home and church, it is especially important for all of us to put aside our "I thinks" and allow God's Word to speak.

Ideas are only as good as their sources. It is possible that the interpretation we are familiar with has been only some speaker's or teacher's "I think." But when we let God speak, having had our minds cleared of our own preconceived ideas, we receive from Him exactly what He wants to teach us—the method He wants to use to change us.

Sometimes we even back up our "I thinks" with Scripture that we feel supports our own ideas. "The heaven, even the heavens, are the Lord's; but the earth hath He given to the children of men" (Ps. 115:16) was a verse used by many to prove that man was confined to this planet in the solar system and that he would never be able to land on the moon or any other planet. But this "I think" idea was shattered on July 20, 1969, at 10:56 Eastern Daylight Time, when Neil Armstrong uttered the now almost immortal words "That's one small step for man; one giant leap for mankind." He was the first, but not the last, human to walk on the moon. This process of disproving one's "I thinks" and proving the Bible has been going on for centuries.

Galileo, the seventeenth-century scientist, believed the now-accepted fact that the earth is not the center of the universe. But in 1633 the church forced him to kneel down and, with his hand upon the Gospel, renounce his belief because of what "they thought."

Sometimes we superimpose a change on others because of what we think the Scripture means. I remember being told of a minister, who ran a home for displaced children and young people, having sexual relations with the teenage girls in his care. He firmly believed he was doing the right thing because he thought they needed to experience love (a good scriptural concept). These girls were changed because of his "I think," but certainly not according to the kind of love God would have used to change them. This type of "I think" is spelled S-I-N in God's Word.

How Smart Are You?

While I was being entertained as the guest of honor at a dinner party in a large Southern city, a young man trained in handwriting analysis suddenly asked me, "What's your IQ?"

All conversation ceased as those around me listened for my answer. "Sorry, no way am I going to talk about that," I replied, embarrassed at the silence.

I suddenly realized he meant business and was ready to tell me all he knew. "OK, I'll tell you how smart I am." He smiled a little "I won" grin as all eyes focused on me. Slowly and very deliberately I said, "I'm smart enough to know that I don't know" (I could almost feel the shocked silence). "But," pointing upward, toward God in heaven, I added, "I'm also smart enough to know who does know." Proverbs 3:5–6 says: "Trust in the Lord with all thine heart; and lean not unto thine own understanding. In all thy ways acknowledge Him, and He shall direct thy paths." Yes, I know I don't know how to direct my own life. When I lean on my own understanding, I become more and more stubbornly entrenched in my own ambitions, rights, and ideas.

How, then, can I avoid getting my lifestyle from wisdom that is within myself—a source that produces bitter envyings, strife, confusion, and every evil work (James 3:16)? In Proverbs 3:5–6 God has promised that if I *don't* lean on my own understanding, He will take over and direct my paths. Then He will teach me through Bible study, guide me through devotional reading, and recall Scripture when I need it. And He will give me wisdom when I admit I need it and ask Him for it—wisdom that changes me according to His perfect will.

10

Source of Wisdom No. 2— Earthly Wisdom

*"And my speech and my preaching was not with
enticing words of man's wisdom, but in
demonstration of the Spirit and of power:
That your faith should not stand in the wisdom
of men, but in the power of God."*

1 CORINTHIANS 2:4–5

*A*nother source of wisdom by which I am changed that James 3:15 mentions is *earthly*. This is not that which attacks me with fiery darts from Satan's emissaries, nor my own "I thinks" welling up from deep within my sensual self, but it is the wisdom that bombards from the world around me. This is the constant barrage of communicated suggestions that pellet me from every angle: people, books, newspapers, radio, and television. The parade is endless and unrelenting. Bit by bit they push, press, chisel, and invade until I am changed—unsuspectingly—into a composite of their messages.

The advertising media have learned the power contained in suggestions that flash so rapidly on my TV screen. I am not even aware of them, but I am motivated to get up out of my chair and go to the kitchen for something to eat or to go out and buy their product. These hidden persuaders are not only on TV; they are subtly at work on me all day long from a myriad of sources.

In Romans 12:2 Paul refers to the results of this process as *conforming* to the world. He writes, "And be not conformed to this world." To conform is to become similar to, to bring into harmony or agreement with, to act in accordance with. CHANGED! Changed to conform to what? The *world*. The age in which we live—the principles and practices of this present order of things—becomes our source of wisdom which in turn changes us into conformity to it. Paul warns us against this. James says that this wisdom "descendeth not from above [from God], but is earthly" (3:15).

Peter puts it this way: "Wherefore gird up the loins of your mind ... as obedient children, not fashioning yourselves according to the former lusts in your ignorance" (1 Peter 1:13–14). What are these former lusts? Paul defines them in Ephesians 2:1–3: "And you [Christians] hath He quickened, who were dead in trespasses and sins; Wherein in time past ye walked according to the course of this world, according to the prince of the power of the air, the spirit now worketh in the children of disobedience; Among whom also we all had our conversation [way of life] in times past in the lusts of our flesh, fulfilling the desires of the flesh and of the mind; and were by nature the children of wrath even as others."

BOMBARDED BY A RELENTLESS PARADE

What becomes commonplace changes me. I can remember the times when I hurt inside if anyone took God's name in vain, when I winced at some of the four-letter words so commonly used on TV today—words I never allowed to enter my home by any other way. I never tolerated a child's playmate or a crude adult friend using those words, but now I am completely unaware of the vile language so casually used on the TV in my family room.

And God's standard for marriage is steadily eroding as the ever-present marriage triangle on TV now involves not just the bad guy but our heroes, the "nice guys." Sleeping overnight with someone else's wife or husband doesn't carry a hint that it might be wrong. Soap operas constantly feature the third person in the marriage relationship, and on one program a divorced mother talks freely to her two daughters about not "doing it" until "Mr. Right" comes along. And little by little we are a bit less shocked as we grow accustomed to that kind of lifestyle.

In today's popular music there has crept in a gradual changing of moral values. We find ourselves actually sympathizing with the lovers who have to keep their "beautiful" love a secret till they both are free from the selfish culprits to whom they are married. And the young woman alone in her room at night convincingly laments that there is some man out there missing what she has to give.

I recall the startled expression on the face of a member of my Sunday School class when we read Jesus' words in Matthew 5:28 that "whosoever looketh on a woman to lust after her hath committed adultery with her already in his heart." Horrified, he exploded, "Does it really say that?" Yes, God's "flee fornication" still stands, no matter how much the world tries to change our thinking.

I wonder how many Christian young people are getting their moral standards from this relentless parade, and how many adults unwittingly lower their ideals because of this invasion by the world. And when does turning our heads and ignoring it change into condoning? *Changed*—first in our thinking then in our actions.

GULLIBLE—IF IT'S IN PRINT

A returned missionary shared with me that he felt God was calling him to translate good literature to send to the nationals he had just left. "They believe anything that is in print," he lamented. But it happens here in America, too. A national denominational women's executive said to me one day, "What can we do about the gullibility of our women? Now that women are 'thinking for themselves' they are reading and studying everything they can get their hands on. And they are believing anything, as long as it's in print, swallowing everything printed under the name of 'Christian.'"

We should test every book we read by the Bible's standards, but the tendency today is to make the Bible's teachings fit into those of a book—secular or religious. In a Sunday School class a teacher was using a popular secular book, attempting to conform biblical concepts to the ideas expressed in the book. After a few sessions of this study, a doctor's wife became extremely agitated and said, "I personally studied this material in a seminar conducted by the author, and by 9 A.M. he was 'bombed.' And we Christians are evaluating the Bible by what this alcoholic's book says!" Many of us act as if the Bible is on trial, whereas we should judge every book by what the Bible says. And this includes Christian books. An internationally known Christian psychologist startled me one day when he said that he didn't know a single Christian book that did not have in it something he considered to be contrary to the Scripture.

And we must evaluate *all* the teachings in a book. A national Christian radio personality told me that she had been reprimanded for reviewing a certain book on the air. In her hurried perusal of that book, she missed the one anti-scriptural teaching in it. But she learned that it was necessary to check out all the teachings of any book before she reviewed it. I've heard people say in defense of an author, "But that book has so much good in it." Great. Take what is good and true and accept it. But we must reject anything, even from our favorite author, that is not consistent with biblical truth. A lot of truth in a book doesn't automatically make everything in the book true.

SOURCE OF WISDOM WHEN WE TEACH

Discerning an author's source of wisdom is also wise. When an author has been taught by God, what he has written can be a valuable source of wisdom for my changing. But I must be alert to things in print which are a result of the author's having received wisdom from Satan's realm or from his own "I thinks." If the teachings in a book are contrary to the Scriptures, the source of the author's wisdom could not have been from God, but from one of the other three sources—sensual self, demonic, or earthly.

Many times our preconceived ideas, our "I thinks" about what we want the Scriptures to say, color our interpretation. I was appalled as I read a Christian couple's paraphrase of Proverbs 31 in a Christian magazine. It obviously was their idea of the perfect wife, but it had little to do with the actual description of the virtuous woman recorded in the Bible portion. They wrote, "Your own clothing will be modest, but chosen in colors to please your husband," while the Bible actually said she made herself coverings of tapestry and her clothing was silk and purple (v. 22). And they said, "There may be many beautiful and intelligent women in the world, but I wouldn't trade you for any of them," whereas the Bible says the virtuous woman opens her mouth with wisdom (v. 26). Again they wrote of her buying fresh fruits and vegetables and, in consultation with her family, organizing the day's responsibilities. But the Bible said she considers a field and buys it—an independent businesswoman (v. 16). And the purpose of her making fine linen and girdles was to sell them to the merchants—not only for her family. This virtuous woman must have been an intelligent and clever businesswoman, for even civic leaders in the gates praised her for her work.

A pastor's wife recently said to me, "I get that doctrine all straightened out until I go back and read so-and-so again." How easy it is to accept gullibly some author's "I think" about the Bible and be changed by it, not stopping to test it by what the Scripture actually says. But wisdom is only as good as the author's source, and is only worthy as a source of change for us if God has been his teacher.

Several years ago a teacher at a parent-teacher night said that our first-grade child had picked a book from the school library which she, a Christian teacher, questioned. Knowing we were a preacher's family, she said, "Oh, honey, you don't want to read *that* book, to you?" "Well," was the reply, "we don't have to believe everything we read." Did that little first-grader know something many adults have not yet learned? Do we accept without question and are we changed by anybody's printed wisdom regardless of its source?

Those of us who write and teach have a grave responsibility to make sure of our source of wisdom. To admit we are wrong and change our teaching is admirable; but in doing so we must admit that our former source of wisdom could not have been from God for it expressed an opposing view.

This puts an awesome responsibility on my shoulders to make sure that *before* I teach others my source of wisdom has not been my "I thinks"—the results of being squeezed into the world's mold, or the contemporary Christian culture, or by what is acceptable thinking and behavior in my specific Christian community. Or that my teaching has not been colored by the sensual welling up from within me. The really frightening responsibility is to make sure my source is not from demons. Satan can appear as an angel of light (2 Cor. 11:14), and some of his subtle persuaders look so right and feel so good that I sometimes have trouble catching those deceptions. But if I pass those on as I teach, they become heresy. I'm sure most anti-scriptural teaching is done in complete innocence, the teacher having been convinced that his or her source of wisdom was God. But Paul warns us in 2 Corinthians 2:11 that we are not to be ignorant of Satan's scheming ways.

Then the question comes, *how can we retract and correct teaching that we have received from the three sources of wisdom other than God?* I may be able to reach a few, but the seeds I have sown multiply and in turn are scattered by those I have taught. How imperative it becomes for me to pray *before* I teach, asking God to remove all my preconceived ideas which may have been from the other three sources, and then to ask Him to guard and guide my mind as I study and teach.

There are some excellent books for husbands and wives these days that are God-inspired and tremendously beneficial. There are others that have not been inspired by Him. Here again, the author's source of wisdom makes the difference—God's holy Word or Hollywood. Is it advice that will change me into what God wants me to be? One husband complained to me, "My wife is acting like God is the Hugh Hefner of the sky." Also, where the author is in his or her personal life at a given point in time may not be the direction God wants us to take. We may be changed—but not according to God's will! Someone may be "teaching for doctrines the commandments of men" (Mark 7:7).

TEST BY WHAT IT PRODUCES

Inadequate Bible study and basing our teaching on an inaccurate premise of what we think the Bible says produces the wrong kind of changes in our lives. Many women have come to me angry, depressed, or in tears because they studied material that was not accurate according to the Scripture, and they had tried to change into persons God did not intend them to be.

An extremely frustrated and guilt-ridden author and teacher came to me one day because what she taught a woman had produced a husband who, instead of becoming the head of the house, had taken a gun and blown his brains out. Silently, I questioned the source of wisdom resulting in such tragedy. Reading through just the first six pages of her study course, I found a long list of things that I did not believe were scriptural, including the basic premise of the whole study. I went to prayer asking God to reveal the mind of Christ to her—not what Evelyn thinks, for I can be right *or wrong*, and what God is saying to me for my life might not be what He is saying to her for hers.

If our new lifestyle produces rebellion in our mates, it is good to check the source of wisdom that is affecting our changing. One husband whose wife had been following step-by-step a course of study finally exploded, "Honey, I married you because you were a bubbly, outgoing, beautiful hostess. I loved you the way you were. Will you please stop this idiotic behavior? I can't stand you this way." The changes in her life had infuriated him. And many husbands have been insulted and embarrassed that men in their social circles or neighborhood have all been receiving the same planned treatment each week. Discovering that their friend's wives and their own were changing their behavior toward their husbands in exactly the same way has caused deep hurts.

If what we teach produces bitterness, confusion, guilt, embarrassment, rebellion, insult, or even divisions among Christians, we need to check the source of wisdom from which we are deriving our teaching. James 3:17 and 18 tell us: "But the wisdom that is from above is first pure, then peaceable, gentle, and easy to be entreated, full of mercy and good fruits, without partiality, and without hypocrisy. And the fruit of righteousness is sown in peace by them that make peace."

NOT TO MANIPULATE

My motive for changing is not to manipulate other people. When I pray,

"Lord, change me" I am only concerned with my changing into what He wants *me* to be. Peter said my changed actions and attitudes will *affect* the people around me. Others will change as they see and observe my "chaste and reverent behavior" (1 Peter 3:1–2), but God takes care of changing them. I am responsible for me.

Some of the books and studies for women these days are designed to manipulate the husband into a certain response when the wife follows a certain pattern of behavior. One course of study teaches the wife how to manipulate her husband so that she with him will qualify for a higher place in heaven. And another study switches from God's plan to that of movie stars for manipulating men, husband or not.

One man said to me recently, "I am insulted that my wife is trying to manipulate my behavior in this way."

God's Word abounds with instructions for both husband and wife which are sufficient to produce all the joys, privileges, and beauty of the marriage relationship. Letting God change us into warm, loving, responsive mates physically, emotionally, and spiritually is His will for us—not manipulation of one another, but for each to be changed into what He wants us to be. Paul says in Colossians 2:8, "Beware lest any man spoil you through philosophy and vain deceit, after the tradition of men, after the rudiments of the world, and not after Christ."

SQUEEZED INTO THEIR MOLD

One of the ways we conform to this world is described in J.B. Phillips' version of Romans 12:2 "Don't let the world around you squeeze you into its own mold."

We are exposed these days to courses of study that would squeeze us into the mold of the world. Many of these courses, in the areas of mind expansion, philosophy, and social behavior, are strictly from a worldly perspective with no consideration as to God's teachings. In them a clever, persuasive teacher can present the material in such a way that it produces dramatic changes in thinking and actions—frequently opposite from God's way of changing.

We tend to believe a teacher if he or she draws a large crowd. And we instinctively feel all those people can't be wrong. But as I read through the text of Mr. Sun Myung Moon's speech given to the standing-room-only crowd at Madison Square Garden, I realized the error of this thinking. He cleverly twisted and misinterpreted Scripture to "prove" that Jesus did not come to earth to die, the cross was not God's will for Christ, the Crucifixion was a mistake, and Jesus thus could not save us totally. Then he went on to "prove" that Jesus was not coming back in the clouds but would be born again as the third Adam in the flesh.

A few years ago, a distraught leader of a large denominational district rally told me her daughter had left home to live at Mr. Moon's head-quarters. After I spoke to their gathering on this subject, the denomination's leader stood up and said, "I hope you paid attention to Mrs. Christenson, for right now, these Moon representatives will most like-ly knock on your door. It is our community they are saturating this week with their philosophy." Moon's followers are missionaries to Christians—trying to squeeze us into their mold. Trying to change us—but not as God would have us change. God's Word says, "Let no man deceive you with vain words" (Eph. 5:6).

ADVICE FROM OTHER PEOPLE

As a young pastor's wife in our first city pastorate 40 years ago, I was eager to please everybody, and slacks to some Christians were still question-able attire for women. But on our first Christmas in that pastorate my mother-in-law gave me a pair of lovely maroon wool slacks. I immediately put them on to go to the train station to meet an arriving relative. Just as I stepped out our front door, an elderly member of our church passed by, stuck her nose in the air and said, "Harumph. Women in pants!" Then strode defiantly on past our house in the howling wind. Should I rush back and change into a skirt and be late for the train—or chance it?

As I stood on the train platform with the winter storm raging about and the plaid of my new slacks getting louder by the minute, I suddenly shrank back into the shadows. Another female member of our church! But I was too late. She bounded over to me and sighed, "Well, at last we have a pastor's wife with enough sense to dress for the weather!" Which one was right? Which one's reaction should I heed? It couldn't be both. In my confused state I dug out my Bible and once again found the answer from God—Acts 5:29: "We ought to obey God rather than men [people]."

One Christmas my husband and I sat looking at the family picture on the Christmas card from our former assistant pastor, commenting on what a lovely family they were. He had become the assistant to a successful national leader of thousands of people. "Oh to think I advised him not to go with that man," recalled Chris. (At the time Chris gave that advice that new boss was a relatively unheard-of youth leader.) "That's why we obey God rather than men," I commented.

I remember crying after receiving some advice from another person at a retreat. In a little exercise of giving something to each other she said to me, "I give you a spirit of adventure."

I was crushed. "Lord," I prayed, "have I missed it that much that people think I need a spirit of adventure?" Reviewing that very month, I realized how wrong that advice had been. I had turned fifty—which in itself took a lot of courage. I enrolled in my first seminary class, started speaking on "The Dangers of the Occult," a then very misunderstood subject in churches and schools, organized my first St. Paul telephone prayer chain, conceived and planned the first of the annual Founder's Week luncheons for women at our college and seminary—and on the list went.

I'm sure I needed advice, but a spirit of adventure was not it. I could have used, "Learn to say no," "One thing at a time," or, "Try eight hours of sleep some night." But a spirit of adventure—hardly. I'm sure the advice was well-intended, but missed my real need completely. Psalm 118:8 says, "It is better to trust in the Lord than to put confidence in man." Advice from other people can chisel away at us until we are reduced to a fraction of all that God intended us to be. God's wisdom enlarges, matures, and fulfills us.

However, the worth of people's advice is determined by their source of wisdom. There is much Christian counseling that is worthwhile and beneficial. But all advice must be evaluated in the light of the advice God gives in His Word. If the counseling is contrary to the Bible's instructions or from the person's "I thinks" it can never change us into the person God intends us to be. "And my speech and my preaching was not with enticing words of man's wisdom, but in demonstration of the Spirit and of power; that your faith should not stand in the wisdom of men, but in the power of God" (1 Cor. 2:4–5).

How precious is the counsel of the godly to us, and how good to be changed by it; but even Job (Job 38:1–2), Christ (Matt. 16:21–23), and Peter and John (Acts 4:18–20) had to firmly reject being changed by the advice from people so that they could follow God's instructions and leading in their lives.

Changed? Yes! But by the only infallible, consistently reliable Source—the Lord.

11

Source of Wisdom No. 3— From Demons

"This wisdom descendeth not from above, but is earthly, sensual, devilish"

JAMES 3:15

*A*s I discovered, in James 3:15 that Sunday morning, the four sources of wisdom by which I could be changed, the most horrifying one to me was the wisdom from demons. Although I was well aware of this subject doctrinally, the sudden realization that it was possible for me to receive and be changed by wisdom from demons completely unnerved me.

Then I began to wonder. How much of the "confusion, strife, bitterness, and evil work" in my life have been caused by an input from Satan's kingdom? The possibility of demons literally shaping my lifestyle by the wisdom they were giving me suddenly loomed as a dark, threatening menace. I thought of the anger over that remark made years before that had seemed to come from nowhere as I read my Bible that morning. God had forgiven, and when He forgives, He forgets. So who dug up something settled nine years ago? Not God! I looked at the other three sources. Not the earthly source from other people—I was alone in my living room. My own "I think"? I couldn't make any sense out of that one since the incident hadn't been a part of my thinking, at least not that I was aware of, for nine years. I was left with just one source of wisdom that was producing that un-Christ-like attitude in me—a supernatural source from demons!

SPIRIT OF DISCERNMENT

One evening we had taken Corrie ten Boom to dinner at the top of the IDS tower in Minneapolis. Ignoring the breathtaking view across our city, she suddenly asked, "What is the gift of the Holy Spirit least sought after these days by Christians?" Several shook their heads, not knowing what Corrie was going to say. "I think I may know, Corrie," I said. "Is it a spirit of discernment?" (1 Cor. 12:10) Her eyes lit up. "Yes!" And she was off on one of her wonderful little sermonettes on a subject about which she was feeling deeply.

God had shown me this three years before in 1 Corinthians 12:8 and 10, "For to one is given by the Spirit ... discerning of spirits." At that time I had prayed that He would give me that gift, the ability to identify the source—which spirit it was that was producing my lifestyle and that of others.

Then Corrie said, "It's a poor soldier, indeed, who doesn't even recognize the enemy."

Peter recognized and discerned the source of wisdom that caused Ananias to lie: "Why hath Satan filled thine heart to lie to the Holy Spirit?" (Acts 5:3)

Perhaps Peter recognized this source so easily because Jesus had identified it in him when Peter in his rebellion declared that Jesus could not go to Jerusalem to die—doing His Father's will (Matt. 16:22–23). Just saying, "I don't believe that can happen to a Christian" doesn't change the truth of our enemy's tactics one bit. The Bible says we do receive wisdom from demons.

Yes, the gift of the Holy Spirit least sought but so needed these days is the gift of discerning the spirits—the gift which enables us to discover the sources of wisdom that will change us and to avoid those which will certainly not change us into being more like Jesus.

BY WHAT IT PRODUCES

I learned from that passage in James 3 that I can identify and discern the source of wisdom by what it produces. Bitter envyings, strife, confusion, and every evil work are always the input of Satan's kingdom. How frequently I have to claim God's "sound mind" of 2 Timothy 1:7, when I find this state of confusion in me, and let God change me!

I also discovered that *fear* is another product of this demonic source of wisdom. Several years ago, while reading our Bibles together until God spoke, another woman and I were puzzled as to why God stopped us both at 2 Timothy 1:7. I tucked this truth down in my heart, but didn't need it until the following September. While conducting a retreat near Banff in the foothills of the Canadian Rockies, I was to speak on Sunday morning on the subject of victory over Satan. The night before, our campfire sharing time near the isolated horse corral was broken up by a pack of wild wolves. Terrified, we had fled to the lodge. Then around midnight when I returned to my bedroom in the far corner of the lodge a sense of uncanny fear came over me. I felt I was not alone, though a thorough search in closets and under the beds revealed no one. Turning out all the lights except the one over my bed, I took my Bible, zipped up my sleeping bag, and began quoting 2 Timothy 1:7: "For God hath not given us the spirit of fear, but of power, and of love, and of a sound mind." Then, telling Satan to get out of the room (James 4:7) and claiming 1 John 4:4, I went to sleep—a beautiful, restful sleep. I awoke the next morning changed, with actual tears of joy in my eyes. Completely changed by recognizing the source of that fear—and claiming that 2 Timothy 1:7 Scripture God had given to me six months earlier.

I saw this fear displayed in a college student from the University of Montana who was sitting next to me on a plane flying to California. He was telling me how deeply he was into meditation.

"Tell me, do you ever hear anything?" I asked.

With fear in his eyes that I cannot describe, he said, "Lady, if I'd tell
you everything I've heard, they'd come with a straitjacket and take me
away. I hear bells, voices … " and with that his voice trailed off. It was-
n't hard for me to discern the source of that fearful lifestyle, but he was-
n't interested in changing it.

As I teach young people on this subject, I can usually tell which ones
are getting their wisdom from some supernatural source other than God
by the peculiar fear they exhibit. As many share their problem quite read-
ily with me, I show them from the Bible that this way of life is not from
God. What a joy to watch them change as they pray, asking God to forgive them. And I know the change is complete when the big smiles spread
over their faces, demonstrating their happiness and relief.

TEST THE SPIRITS

Now for the question: "How can we tell which kind of spirit is changing us?"

The Apostle John gave us a good test of the spirits: "Dear friends, do
not believe every spirit, but test the spirits to see whether they are from
God, because many false prophets have gone out into the world. This
is how you can recognize the Spirit of God: Every spirit that acknowl-
edges that Jesus Christ has come in the flesh is from God; but every spirit that does not acknowledge Jesus is not from God" (1 John 4:1–3, NIV).

John warned us not to believe every spirit; not to accept wisdom from
those that are not of God, not to be changed by what they teach, say, or
suggest to us.

And we are to test them according to whether or not they confess that
Jesus Christ came in the flesh, that is, He took on a body with flesh and
blood for the purpose of shedding that blood on the cross to defeat Satan
(1 John 3:8). Every spirit that does not confess that Jesus is come in the
flesh is not of God.

God said in His Word that "without shedding of blood there is no forgiveness" (Heb. 9:22, NASB). But because Jesus did come in the flesh, He
redeemed us from sin by shedding His blood on the cross. "Forasmuch
as ye know that ye were not redeemed with corruptible things … but with
the precious blood of Christ" (1 Peter 1:18–19). (See also Matt. 26:28;

Col. 1:14; Eph. 1:7.)

Sometimes it's difficult to discern what people who receive wisdom from demons really think of Jesus. A woman in our area, a popular speaker at local occult conventions, supposedly receives messages from dead loved ones by automatic writing. Our local newspaper quoted her as saying that God was great, the great Creator, etc., but farther down in the long article she was quoted as saying, "But the confusion comes when we try to put a *body* on 'it.' God can be an 'it' force in the universe, but don't put a body on 'it.'" Jesus said in John 8:44 that Satan was a liar and the father of lies. This reveals what she thinks of Jesus having come in the flesh!

I was hoping someone dressed in a colonial costume would approach me at the Philadelphia airport when I was there on July 6, just two days after our 1976 bicentennial birthday, and I was not disappointed. A lovely young girl in a bonnet and a long dress started telling me about our country's spiritual heritage. I beamed back and said, "Yes, I love God, and love serving His Son Jesus." At that she gave me a long speech about how great a teacher Jesus was and how wonderful He was. As I nodded in agreement, she continued, "And He was one of the ways to God." I blinked and started to listen more closely. "Oh, yes, He was *one of the ways to God.* There are many ways to God. Let me tell you about mine. I'm a Hare Krishna girl ... "

"Hold it, honey," I interrupted. "I think you are doing a very diabolical thing here in Philadelphia at this, our nation's birthday celebration. Our country was founded on belief in God through Jesus, and you are saying how great He was and at the same time that He is just one of the ways to God. But Jesus said of Himself, 'I am the Way, the Truth, and the Life: no man cometh unto the Father, but by Me' (John 14:6). Now, He is either a barefaced liar, or He is who He said He is—the *only* way to God." What the Hare Krishna followers think of Jesus!

Krishna, whom she follows, says in chapter ten of the *Bhagavad Gita,* "I am the prince of demons." Test the source of that kind of wisdom before believing and being changed by it.

Sometimes it is difficult to test the spirits. Three people supposedly dressed in costumes such as Abraham and Sarah might have worn came to one of my prayer seminars. They would not let me touch them as I tried to shake their hands in welcome because, they said, they were from Am.

"Where's Am?" I asked.

Surprised by my ignorance, they replied, "Oh, that's heaven. God sent us to earth, and He has been saying 'Evelyn' to us. When we saw the sign for your prayer seminar in front of this church, we knew you were the Evelyn."

I immediately started to pray for protection and discernment. (Several others in the audience sensed the need and prayed also.) After the seminar the female of the trio threw her arms around me to give me "a double portion of God's power" because, she said, I had taught everything that night that God had sent them to earth to tell. Perhaps I'll never know the source of those three, but I immediately knew and sensed the protection of Jesus Christ.

DOCTRINE OF DEMONS

False teaching seems to be taking on a new dimension these days. The investigation of inner space and outer space (not authentic exploration) is producing a new kind of wisdom. It's possible to listen to lectures by "beings" from outer space, browse through endless shelves of do-it-yourself inner exploration, attend teaching sessions on the power of the mantra, reincarnation, dreams and the inner world, and astrology as cosmic patterning. Or we can bask in the Caribbean sun on a yoga vacation with a swami or retreat to a Buddhist monastery in the Catskills.

A University of Chicago anthropologist claims 20 million Americans belong to "fringe religious cults" such as the Hare Krishna movement, spiritualism, and Scientology. The market is flooded these days with cheap or expensive ways of changing with "wisdom" from every source mentioned in James 3 except the true God in heaven.

Paul warns us against the *doctrine of demons*, in 1 Timothy 4:1: "The Spirit explicitly says that, in later times some will fall away from the faith, paying attention to deceitful spirits and doctrines of demons (NASB)." This is not the doctrine *about* demons, but the doctrine *of* demons.

After a recent prayer seminar a woman in her twenties said to me, "I was deeply into TM, but recently while meditating I heard a voice say, 'That is of the devil.' Now, I'm from a church where we never talk about the devil, so that word could not have come from within me. It had to be God." God warning about being changed by the wrong source?

A faculty member of a southern Christian college asked for prayer at a prayer seminar. She had just returned from doing research for a postgraduate dissertation in Iowa near where the Maharishi Mahesh Yogi has established his university. Anxious for all mind-expanding help she could get, she took the TM course and practiced it, but God spoke to her, telling her that this was of Satan and was not for Christians. She immediately renounced the practice. But what she asked us to pray about was that her secret mantra (that Hindu worship word) kept ringing in her head. No matter what she did or how hard she tried, she could not get rid of it. She had been changed in a way she didn't want to be changed.

In one eastern American city, students enrolled in TM classes at their high school brought fruit and flowers to be placed on the altar before the picture of the late Guru Dev. Then, kneeling at this ceremony, they were given a mantra, the secret word that must be repeated to aid meditation.

These students were being changed, not by their own "I think" but by other people whose source of wisdom was not the God above. They were being changed by worshipping a pagan god.

Jesus said this method of meditation is used by pagans when they pray. But He told His disciples, "But when ye pray, use not vain repetitions as the pagans do" (Matt. 6:7, SCO). Repeating one word over and over is not a method Jesus would use to change us.

However, there are biblical methods of meditating on our God who is in heaven. The Scriptures abound with examples. Dr. Herbert Benson, cardiologist and assistant professor of medicine at the Harvard Medical School discovered that, although meditating with a Hindu mantra did beneficially lower blood pressure, meditation in ordinary ways without a secret religious word also produced the same beneficial results. Christians call it prayer. The danger comes not from meditating, but from the spiritual powers to which we open our minds.

A professor in one of our large theological seminaries said, "If you want to find demons today, go to the pulpits of churches on Sunday morning." I questioned the possibility of such a thing until I heard a sermon based on the bestseller, *Jonathan Livingston Seagull*. Although the author himself speaks freely of occult healing power (having actually stopped the flow of blood with supernatural power when he cut himself) and a "voice" telling him what to write in the book, his philosophy was used as a basis for many sermons. And one local pastor leads a group in "healing from the cosmos" every Tuesday evening. At 11 P.M. they meditate and get vibrations from their California headquarters, giving them power and the ability to see auras around people. Are preachers immune to this source of wisdom, or are they *unusually* vulnerable because their wisdom influences so many other people?

A few years ago, the popular book, *UFO Missionaries Extraordinary*, compiled by Hayden Hewes and Brad Steiger, caused much deception about Jesus' second coming. In an interview with Bo and Peep in chapters 7 and 8, in which these two "people" claimed to have existed before and to have been sent to a woman's womb from the heavenly kingdom by a spacecraft that came close enough to earth to make contact, there are profuse references to Jesus and the Bible. They said they were part of a preparation for Christ's coming. Their teachings sound so plausible and are so near what Christ taught. When Jesus really comes back and Christians are taken up to be with Him, will people remember that book and believe those Christians went to the next level in a space ship?

A fine Christian woman with an important job for God in our area called me and said, "I've just read the *Reader's Digest* condensation of the book *Life After Life* by Dr. Raymond A. Moody, Jr. It's about people who died, left their bodies and then were brought back to life. They all (unless they committed suicide), whether Christian or non-Christian, had such a beautiful experience. There was nothing unpleasant, no judgment, and a warm being of light was seen by most of them. We Christians may have to reevaluate our position on what happens after death in the light of all that evidence!"

Taken aback, I recovered enough to say to her, "You are in a very important position for God in our city right now. You are especially vulnerable. Let me pray about this and I'll get back to you."

While reading that book few days before, I had asked God to guard my mind and give me wisdom as to its truth. After the phone call, I prayed asking God to give me His answer to that book. Immediately the scriptures in Hebrews 9:27 came to mind, "It is appointed unto men once to die, but after this the judgment." I suddenly realized what God was saying, "If those people are back here to tell the story, they did not really die." The death process was not complete. It is after we really die that there will be judgment—and eternal damnation for those who do not know Christ. The whole biblical teaching of the wages of sin being death must be discarded if there is only pleasantness, warmth, and light after death. Jesus said in John 3:16, 18: "For God so loved the world, that He gave His only begotten Son, that whosoever believeth in Him should not perish, but have everlasting life. ... But he that believeth not is condemned already."

The "doctrine of demons" may not be popular with some Christians, but I remember God powerfully saying to me as I was reading 1 Timothy 4:6: "If thou put the brethren in remembrance of these things, thou shalt be a good minister of Jesus Christ." Looking back to see what "these things" were, I realized Paul was talking about the "doctrine *of* demons." I don't like that subject either, but if I put other Christians "in remembrance of these things," God's Word says I will change into a better minister of Jesus Christ.

How We Open Ourselves to Wisdom from Demons

"Where did we go wrong?" lamented a mother of a college girl who had left her Christian college to enroll in and later become a teacher in a local school for witches. I'm sure this is the question being asked by many agonizing and anxious parents. There are many ways Christians can open themselves to wisdom from demons, sometimes without being aware of what is happening.

There is much actual teaching of occult practices in our public schools and universities these days. During a question-and-answer period at a workshop conducted in Washington, D.C., I heard a schoolteacher from a large Florida city ask what could be done about the occult practices that were being taught in public grade schools by immigrants who brought their voodoo and witchcraft practices with them to Florida.

And a public school administrator in another large city told me she was terrified that we would get prayer legalized again in schools. She told me that she knows personally Satan worshipers and witches who are teaching in their schools and added that in a democracy if Christians get the right to lead their pupils in prayer, so will the Satan worshipers and witches. And, she said, if our children are exposed to that kind of praying year after year, I'm not sure we'd ever recover them.

A distraught mother told our prayer chain chairman that the people of the movement "The Way" were teaching her daughter that she should follow them if she wanted to be like Jesus, because He disobeyed His parents when He was twelve. That wisdom didn't come from God. They were seeking to change that little girl to be just the opposite of what the Bible says about obeying parents.

"Why did God stop all eighteen of us individually on the word 'sorcery' in our cabin as we were reading Galatians 5 until He spoke?" asked a retreat chairman. "You had better tell *me* why," I answered. Then came a startling discussion of how they were using occult practices, such as Ouija boards, for advice in their farming procedures. Wisdom from God? In prayer those women confessed this as sin. God changed them by stopping them all on the same, very frightening word—sorcery!

Sometimes we deliberately ask for wisdom from demonic sources. Perhaps the most common way these days is by reading *horoscopes.* Millions of Americans get their daily lifestyle from the newspaper columns. God forbade this ancient practice, along with many other occult practices that are prevalent today, in instructions to Moses as the Children of Israel were entering the Promised Land. God said that those who do such things are an abomination to Him (Deut. 18:9–12).

At a retreat we were attending, a pastor's wife became concerned because there weren't any newspapers available. "I won't know how to run my life today," she moaned. "I won't be able to read my horoscope." Being susceptible to the power of suggestion from a source God calls an abomination to Him is dangerous indeed. And it certainly can't lead us in the direction God would have us go.

Believing and following predictions of psychics is another way of getting wisdom from a source other than God. We are warned, in Deuteronomy 18:21–22, that unless everything which is prophesied comes to pass, that prophet is not of God. Check the percentage of accuracy! The *National Enquirer's* article of July 6, 1976, revealing the predictions of ten leading psychics for the second half of 1976, included information that Castro would be ousted; Frank Sinatra was to emerge as a national hero after foiling an assassination attempt; Billy Graham would suffer a heart attack forcing him to end his career; a gigantic earthquake in California would tear apart entire mountain ranges revealing the biggest gold deposits ever discovered—all before the end of 1976! Looking back all those years and they still haven't happened. Yet we gullibly swallow and mold our life-patterns by that source of wisdom!

In the past, a frightening number of our children and young people were opening themselves up to wisdom from demons through occult practices. Students in a Christian school were disrupting their school playing Mary Worth—calling forth this witch's image on mirrors in darkened restrooms. At their parents' request, I explained to them that the people who practice this (and get wisdom from Ouija boards, tarot cards, seances, and all the other methods they told me they were using) are an abomination to God. How those students changed that day after I talked to them and as they asked God, one by one in audible prayer, to forgive and deliver them from this!

A mother told me that her daughter had solved a slumber party occult practice. She discovered that the other girls had no power when she prayed. And when they found out that she was the cause of their "games" not working, they wouldn't allow her in the room when they were practicing them.

Another mother told me her daughter worried for years over a palm reader's prediction that she would die by the time she was sixteen. Wisdom from Satan's hierarchy.

Satan engineers our behavior without violating our free will. Weeping, an eighteen-year-old Christian girl told me she had given her body for Satan worship with all its obscene acts because she was dating a boy who was involved in it. At that time, a pain had come in the pit of her stomach, and she had not been able to get through to God in prayer or understand anything in the Bible. After breaking up with the boy and renouncing Satan worship, she tried desperately to free herself from Satan's clutches and these symptoms, but could not. I prayed for her, using the same simple words Jesus prayed in His High Priestly Prayer in John 17, "Dear Father, deliver this dear one from the evil one." Then, according to James 4:7, I just said, "Satan, in the name of Jesus of Nazareth, get out of this dear girl."

The change was instantaneous and dramatic. She grabbed her throat as if choking, became a little lightheaded, and then jumped up and threw her arms around me. "It's gone. The pain's gone. I'm free!" Changed by Jesus Christ!

A graduate of a Christian college I know personally was watching a TV program on Satan worship from San Francisco. He foolishly said, "If you're real, Satan, prove it." And Satan did. For over a year, though he struggled against it, power and direction for his life came from voices speaking to him in the shower and through inner compulsions. It is possible to voluntarily open ourselves to direction from Satan's kingdom.

Books on occult practices abound in our best bookstores. Anyone desiring to be changed in this way has only to buy a book describing in detail the method he has chosen. But this is not new. Acts 19:19 tells us, "Many of those also who use [magical] arts brought their books together, and burned them before all men, and they counted the price of them, and found it fifty thousand pieces of silver." A huge sum compared to the worth of our Christ to Judas—sold for *thirty* pieces of silver.

Yes, we do receive wisdom from demons in so many different ways, sometimes by deception, sometimes by unknowingly opening ourselves, and at other times, deliberately. But the results are the same—change into a lifestyle opposite of what God would choose for us.

Keep Your Mind on Jesus

An unusual demonic influence was described to me by a distraught woman in a western city who had fourteen immediate ancestors who were witches. They had practiced voodoo and palm reading on her from the time she was two years old. A pastor had recently cast out the demons, but she was left with what she described as a hole in the pit of her stomach. I had no idea what she was talking about, but promised to meet her the following Saturday. On Thursday morning I awoke early and begged God to give me an answer for her. And He started recalling Scripture—Colossians 3:1–3, "Seek those things which are above, where Christ sitteth on the right hand of God"; Philippians 2:9–11, "That at the name of Jesus every knee should bow"; Ephesians 1:3, "In heavenly places in Christ"; Ephesians 1:19–22, "When He raised Him [Christ] from the dead and set Him at His own right hand in the heavenly places." I jotted the references down in my notebook, and when I met her I said, "The Lord gave me some answers for you out of His Word."

"Great," she said. "He gave me some too."

"Mine are in my notebook. I'll turn it face down on the desk while you tell me what Scriptures He gave you."

"God told me I was to get my mind off those demons and get it on Christ. He gave me Colossians 3:1–3; Philippians 2:9–11; Ephesians 1: 19–22." Exactly the same verses God had given me!

"And the hole in my stomach disappeared too. All week long you have been teaching us how to pray and study the Bible. All you've talked about is Jesus. And the void in the pit of my stomach has been filled with Jesus."

What a change. She started that week confused, bitter, and frightened, but finished it radiating her newfound peace and excitement in Jesus.

In August of 1972 I prayed for the first time, "Lord, keep my mind from the evil one." Jesus prayed this prayer for us in His High Priestly Prayer, "Father, I pray … that Thou shouldest keep them from the evil [one]" (John 17:15).

Also I learned God provides us with the armor to withstand in our battle against these "principalities, powers, rulers of darkness of the world and spiritual wickedness in high places" *in the battlefield of our minds* (Eph. 6:12–18).

When I keep my mind in His Word, the sword of the Spirit, I have the weapons for the battle. One of my favorite verses is 1 John 4:4, "Greater is He that is in you [Christ], than he that is in the world [Satan]." When I am experiencing an onslaught of fiery darts, I quote it, and I immediately change into a victorious—not vanquished—soldier for Jesus. One day, just reading that "Jesus … went about … healing all that were oppressed of the devil" (Acts 10:38), lifted the oppression I had been experiencing.

Kathy Barrow, the beautiful singer sponsored by World Vision, said to me one day as we were talking about this battle, "I know how it comes out." And pointing to her Bible said, "I have read the end of the Book!" (See Rev. 20:10.) Yes, even Satan knows Jesus came to earth to destroy his works (1 John 3:8), and that Jesus said, in Matthew 25:41, "Depart from me, ye cursed, into everlasting fire, prepared for the devil and his angels." And even the demons recognized Jesus as He started His public ministry, crying, "Art Thou come to destroy us? I know Thee, who Thou art, the Holy One of God" (Mark 1:24). Victory in Jesus!

Sometimes I feel my shield of faith needs to be as powerful as the heat shield of a NASA space capsule to quench the fiery darts of Satan. But it never fails because my faith is in a Person, the risen, glorified, Lord Jesus Christ.

All this armor listed in Ephesians 6 is to protect my thought life—to withstand the wisdom of Satan and his emissaries, the demons. But there is no mention of falling, only standing and withstanding when I wear God's armor! James did show us that frightening source of wisdom—from demons. But he also gave us the promise: "Resist the devil, and he will flee from you" (James 4:7).

It is imperative to admit the reality of this source of wisdom and be alert to discern it, but it is equally important to keep it in its proper perspective. It's good to remember the advice the mama spook gave to the baby spook, "Don't spook unless spoken to." Even though "the whole world lies in the power of the evil one" (1 John 5:19, NASB), it is also true that the earth is only God's footstool. This little speck of dust in the universe we call Planet Earth is temporarily Satan's domain, but the heaven of the heavens cannot contain my God (1 Kings 8:27). And He lives in me!

Yes, it is possible for me to be changed when I receive and am changed by wisdom from demons. But this is not a necessary outcome in my life. I have been given all the resources and power I will ever need to resist this source of wisdom and be changed only as God wants me changed— not by the wisdom from Satan but with wisdom from Him.

12

Source of Wisdom No. 4— The LORD

"If any of you lack wisdom, let him ask of God,
that giveth to all men liberally, and upbraideth not;
and it shall be given him."

JAMES 1:5

*A*nd be not conformed to this world; but be ye transformed by the renewing of your mind, that ye may prove what is that good, and acceptable, and perfect, will of God" (Rom. 12:2).

Transformed! The opposite of being conformed to this world!

"Lord, is this what You had in mind when You led me to pray, 'Lord, change me' so many years ago? God, do You mean I can actually be transfigured just as Christ was on the Mount of Transfiguration? (Matt. 17:2) It's the same Greek word, Lord. Really changed like that?

"I guess You meant it, Lord, because You said, 'Be *ye* transformed.'

"You wouldn't have said that if You didn't mean it, Lord. Is this what You've been doing all these years? Transforming me?

"Lord, I know You are the only Source of wisdom worthy to be used to produce my lifestyle, and You've taught me all these ways to obtain Your wisdom; but *how* have You been accomplishing this transformation in me? It's been a huge task, Lord! How have You done it?"

THE SOURCE IS ALSO THE MEANS

We have an oil painting of my husband's favorite verse on one of our walls, and every time I walk by it I am reminded of how the Lord accomplishes this changing, this transforming in me: "For it is *God* who worketh in you both to will and to do of His good pleasure" (Phil. 2:13). The Source of wisdom to change me is also the Means. It is God Himself who is working in me, producing the change. When I try to pick myself up by my own bootstraps I can fall so flat on my face. Even when I know how to change, doing it myself is practically impossible.

But there is a Person involved. A divine Means. Back in November 1971, I wrote "Lord, change me" in the margin of my Bible by Hebrews 11:6, "Without faith it is impossible to please [God]." Then I added, "I believe You will do it." But the faith is not in the seeking or the changing process; faith is in a Person. God will reward me and work in me when I diligently seek Him. God is the divine Means for my changing.

"How, then, Lord, do *You* bring about this changing?"

BY THE RENEWING OF YOUR MIND

How does God accomplish this transformation in our lives? When we accept Christ we become a new creation (2 Cor. 5:17). The Book of Romans was written to those who already had become new creations (1:7); and, according to Romans 12:2, there is a process that should be going on in the lives of these people, for the phrase "be ye transformed" is in the present continuous tense. And these new creations have within them the potential of this ongoing process of being transformed.

These new creations are to be transformed *by the renewing of their minds*—not "in the vanity of their own minds, but by a change in their patterns of thinking" (Eph. 4:17–23). It is in the realm of our thinking that we are bombarded by the three wrong sources of wisdom listed in James 3:15, but it is also in this realm that God does His changing.

Proverbs 23:7 tells us, "For as he thinketh in his heart, so is he." To realize that I am actually the sum total of all that I think is frightening. But it is also exciting, for God is in the continuous process of changing what I think—and thus changing me. He is providing both the wisdom and the means to change my thinking. And the results is a transformed me!

I'M UNIQUE

How I thank God that He created me a unique individual. Nobody else is just like me. And God's finished product, "Me," is different from any other He has planned.

But I realize that every other Christian is unique too and God is changing them according to His divine blueprint. I have a tendency to feel that if some changing is right for me, then God must want everybody else to change in the same way. But that is not true. The way the Lord changes me does not automatically become a pattern for every other person. Only the omniscient God of heaven has clearly in mind the finished product for each of His children, and I must let Him, not Evelyn, be every individual's Source of wisdom. I must direct others to the Designer of their individual blueprint—the Lord of glory.

And having God's unique blueprint in my spiritual genes also makes me responsible; accountable for all the potential He put in me; answerable to God for how I let Him change me into what He ultimately wants me to be. "So then every one of us shall give account of himself to God" (Rom. 14:12).

This places the ultimate responsibility on each individual before God. In the final judgment each person will answer for himself. God has only children, no grandchildren. I will be accountable *only* for me—only for what I have allowed God to do in and through me. "O Lord, change ME!"

CHANGED—SO THAT ...

Change for the sake of change doesn't make much sense. In the natural realm, the new isn't always better than the old. Romans 12:2, however, gives us the reason for our being transformed. And this is not only better but best. "Be ye transformed by the renewing of your mind, *that ye may prove what is that good, and acceptable, and perfect, will of God*" (italics mine). This is that will of God which is in itself pleasing to Him and which results in actions on the part of His children that are pleasing and acceptable to Him. Changed so that all the words of my mouth and the meditations of my heart are *acceptable* in the sight of my Lord (Ps. 19:14). Changed, so that I will be and do what He wants.

Changed, also, that others may observe my behavior—which has been changed because my thinking is acceptable to God (1 Peter 3:1–2). So often our lives reflect "do as I say, not as I do," but the Bible says in 1 Peter that my husband (and other people) are changed and won when they see *my* changed life.

A psychiatrist who attended one of my prayer seminars wouldn't accept anything I said until she saw me in action with other people. Not knowing she could read lips, I questioned her intense gaze from the other side of the room as I interacted with and counseled several different people at a dinner party following the seminar. My speech at the seminar was of little value to her until she saw me prove myself in action. James says a person who is really wise *shows* it out of a good life (3:13).

The first spring we lived in our house in St. Paul, I came down to the dining room one morning to see it alive with brilliant color. The whole room was aglow with little rainbows all over the walls, ceiling and furniture. The rising sun had come far enough north to be directly in line with my small kitchen window, the dining room door and then our crystal chandelier. And the piercing white light of that morning sun was producing hundreds of rainbows of every color of the spectrum by diffusing through all the crystals. I swung the chandelier ever so slightly, and the colors danced and flashed around the room. I stood spellbound at the spectacular sight.

How similar that is to God's penetration of my life. Webster's *New World Dictionary* defines white as "the color of radiated, transmitted, or reflected light containing all of the visible rays of the spectrum." And God too is the sum total of all that exists. He is infinite. One of His attributes is infinity—that quality of being limitless, to which nothing can be added. And He enters me as pure white piercing light. God in me, my

Source of change, wanting to *radiate* through me all the visible rays of the sum total of all that He is. God's acceptable will for me is that I will let Him change me until I sparkle and glow and radiate Him into my whole environment.

THERMOMETER OR THERMOSTAT?

Changed—so that we become a thermostat, not a thermometer.

So much of the time we are like thermometers, registering the temperature of the atmosphere around us. We respond to a cold shoulder, a chilly remark, a cool reception with a plunge of our own thermometers. Or a hot accusation influences us to flash back with a hotter retaliation. We find it difficult to keep cool heads with heated arguments going on around us, and a warm, suggestive look frequently fans into a burning temptation. But when we let God change us into what He wants us to be, we become thermostats—changing the climate around us, not just registering it.

And when it is God who sets the dial our environment always changes for the better. When the suggested change comes from our sensuous self, Satan's kingdom, or from other people, the temperature extreme may get worse instead of better. But when God changes us, a cold piercing glance turns into a tender look, a sharp tongue utters a soft answer, an aloof stance melts into a loving caress, a clenched fist into a squeezing hand.

But we must have complete confidence in the divine Changer. He always knows when the temperature needs changing to better the environment, and He always knows just how many degrees to turn the dial.

MY SPIRITUAL BAROMETER

For over twenty years my spiritual barometer has been 1 John 1:4, "These things write we unto you, that your joy may be full." The amount of time I spend in God's Word, letting Him change me, seems to register on my spiritual personality indicator. The more time I spend seeking after God's wisdom, the more joy He produces in me.

As I grow older I find that fewer things cause a "tingle" in the pit of my stomach. The first snow of winter, bare feet on the first spring grass, the first squeeze of my teenage boyfriend's hand all produced an exhilarating sensation. But these impressions seem to diminish with age. However, there is one thrilling sensation that becomes stronger every year and seems to come more frequently with passing years—the thrill of having God speak to me out of His Word!

God changes me *as* I turn to Him for advice on how to change. Proverbs 2:10–11 is underlined in my Bible: "When wisdom entereth into thine heart, and knowledge is pleasant unto thy soul, discretion shall preserve thee, understanding shall keep thee." In the margin I wrote, "*Pleasant*—not rebelling against or negative to but my spirit soaring in JOY." Yes, God's wisdom is written down for me so that I might be changed—that my joy might be full.

THE NEXT PLATEAU

God always changes me to lift me to a higher level. Sometimes God's changing takes me through hot fires, deep valleys, grief, or suffering; but after a while the "God of all grace" makes me perfect, established, strengthened, and settled (1 Peter 5:10). These unpleasant experiences have prepared me for the next and higher plateaus of my life.

After an extremely deep valley in our family, I recorded in my Bible my cry to God, "O Lord, when is after a while?" But it was exactly a year later that I added the note, "Now is God's after a while! Great joy again!" It had taken a year for God to do His changing in me and turn that difficult circumstance back to normalcy.

When the violent learning season is over, God settles me down—but not where I was before. As I'm changed, according to His will, He places me on the next plateau that He has prepared. There's always an open door and always power to go through it when I am changed into what He wants me to be.

When I prayed, "Lord, make me the kind of wife *You* want me to be," instead of removing my speaking engagements, God did just the opposite. He opened a whole new life of ministry. He had an exciting succession of open doors ready for me (and many since then). And through those fourteen months of searching, letting Him *change me*, God was preparing me for those doors He was waiting to swing wide open for me.

But even going through His open doors sometimes requires sacrifice. A woman in my group on a World Day of Prayer, commenting on "if any of you lack wisdom, let him ask of God" (James 1:5), said, "Sometimes I don't want wisdom. It's easier to sit in a corner and do nothing than to know what to do and then have to do it."

As my advisory boards and I pray through each new door God seems to be swinging open for us, I realize more and more that obedience requires sacrifice. And it involves sacrifice on my husband's part, also. But God always gives more than I give Him. He has rewarded my obedience with more joy, acceptance, and respect for each other than Chris and I have ever known before. And God is changing me bit by bit into becoming more like the virtuous woman in Proverbs 31 of whom it says, "The heart of her husband doth safely trust in her" (v. 11).

FOR MY GOOD

When God gave me my life verse, Romans 8:28, when I was 23, I had no idea how good the things He was working out for me would be. As I look back, I can see so clearly the way He has picked up the shattered glass of my life and carefully fashioned the stained glass window He is now making of me. Lost babies, surgery, heartaches, grief—all have been used by God to change me—and always for the better.

How I thank Him for the privilege of growing older so I can reflect on what He was really doing. And I'm sure I won't begin to understand all of this until it is explained to me in heaven. God, the Source and the Means of my changing, works out all these things that change me—all for my good.

THEREFORE

This morning I was very tired and felt I could not get out of bed to start the day. As I lay there communing with my God, He brought Isaiah 40 to my mind. Reaching for my Bible I was sure it was verses 28 to 31 about our strength being renewed that He wanted me to read. But I started reading at the beginning of that chapter and found something completely different.

My heart soared as I read about my God—*who He is!* Nobody taught

Him. "All nations before Him are as nothing. ... [He] sitteth upon the circle of the earth, and the inhabitants thereof are as grasshoppers ... [He] stretcheth out the heavens as a curtain. ... Lift up your eyes on high, and behold who hath created these things ... the everlasting God, the Lord, the Creator of the ends of the earth, fainteth not, neither is weary. There is no searching of His understanding" (Isa. 40:17–28). I clutched my Bible to my heart as tears came to my eyes. Who He is!

Then I noticed I had written in the margin of my Bible by Isaiah 40, "12/23/71, see Romans 11:36 to 12:2" with "2" underlined several times. Turning to Romans, I discovered that I had written on that same day "12:1, therefore." God had connected these two passages for me way back then.

Now, whenever we see the word "therefore" we look back to see what it is "there for." In Romans 12:1–2 Paul is "therefore" beseeching us to give God our bodies, not to be conformed to this world, and to be transformed by the renewing of our minds. So what is this transforming process "there for"?

Looking back to the four preceding verses I found what it is "there for" —because of *who God* is. And the words are quoted from Isaiah 40! I am to be transformed by the renewing of my mind because of *who* God is.

"O the depth of the riches both of the wisdom and knowledge of God! How unsearchable are His judgments, and His ways past finding out! For who hath known the mind of the Lord? Or who hath been His counselor? Or who hath first given to Him, and it shall be recompensed unto him again? For of Him, and through Him, and to Him, are all things: to whom be glory forever. Amen" (Rom. 11:33–36).

A PROCESS

I wish I could say that I have arrived, but I can't since this word "transformed" in Romans 12:2 isn't a once-for-all happening. It is a *process*. And whenever I feel that I have arrived, or that I am just about what God had in mind for me to be, He starts changing me again. And this process has been going on all my life.

When I was a little girl I longed for God to change me—into an angel. My sister, brother, and I each had a special Christmas tree ornament that was our very own. We could hang it any place we wanted on the tree trunk. Mine was a beautiful angel. And I would hang it on a low branch, way inside, near the tree where it could not be seen except from our favorite, private spots—under the tree. Lying on my back, I spent hours gazing at that lovely, fragile, glass angel and dreaming my favorite dream: "If only I could be an angel!" How I wished I had been made an angel instead of a little girl.

But the words in a song, "Holy, holy, is what the angels sing," that became popular when I was a young teenager, brought it all into focus for me:

"But when I sing redemption's story,
    They will fold their wings;
For angels never knew the joys
    That our salvation brings."

No, created in all their beauty, power, and intelligence, no angels will ever have the privilege I have of being changed by God, step-by-step, into conformity to the image of His dear Son, Jesus (Rom. 8:29). The angels probably aren't going through the often hard, deep and fiery changing process, but neither are they *becoming conformed to Jesus' image*! Nor have they been promised someday *to be like Him*. Yes, they see Him now and have seen Him for eternal ages past, but they are still not like Him. But I, a mere mortal, *when I see Him will be like Him*. "When He shall appear, we shall be like Him" (1 John 3:2). Whether I leave this world through death or am changed "in the twinkling of an eye" when my Jesus returns, the process will be complete.

"Behold, I show you a mystery; we shall not all sleep, but *we shall all be changed*. In a moment, in the twinkling of an eye, at the last trump; for the trumpet shall sound and the dead shall be raised incorruptible, and *we shall be changed*" (1 Cor. 15:51–52).

I shall be perfect as He is perfect! My long "Lord, change me" struggle will be over. I will be like Jesus!

"Dear Father, I have so far to go. I fall so short of what You want me to be. Please keep changing me on this earth until there won't be so much left to change when I see my Jesus. LORD, CHANGE ME!"